BERNARDINE

A COMEDY IN TWO ACTS

BERN

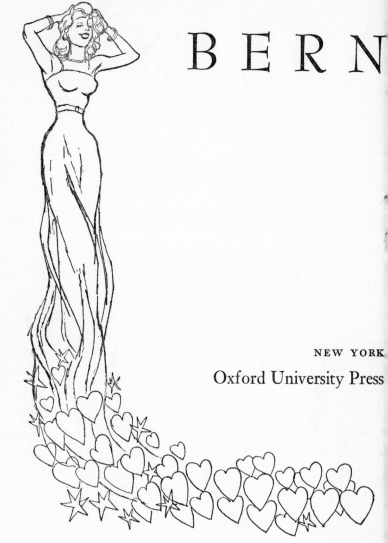

NEW YORK

Oxford University Press

Illustrated by William Sharp

BY MARY CHASE

ARDINE

To Michael Lamont Chase
who not so many years ago was a "big wheel" himself
this book of the play Bernardine *is lovingly dedicated*
by his mother

Introduction

It's quite possible to leave your home for a walk in the early morning air and return a different person—beguiled, enchanted.

This happened to me a few years ago.

I went walking in a park near my home in Denver, Colorado, and found myself looking at the heels of one of the town's most prominent old financiers, taking a turn on the graveled path while his car and chauffeur waited near by.

He had a gold-headed cane and there was a lot of mileage on that cane. It had taken him through many big business mergers and up and down streets named for him. I recognized him only from his pictures in the papers.

Coming toward him now I saw three teen-age boys wearing blue jeans, T shirts, and flattened-out felt hats with feathers stuck in the crown.

"How ya, E.J.?" "What's news, E.J.?" "How are tricks, E.J.?"

The banker spoke to his chauffeur.

"Who are those boys?"

"Nobody at all, sir. Just a bunch of smart alecks. Don't pay any attention to them, sir."

He helped the old man into the car and smoothed a blanket over his knees. But the old man kept turning around and staring after the boys who went striding through the park.

"Those boys knew me all right," he insisted. "I don't know them but they knew ME."

The chauffeur looked after them with scorn but the old man looked after them—I swear it—yearningly, as their long, lithe figures were silhouetted for one instant against the blue sky with the bluer Rockies beyond. Then they were gone. And it was this which caught and held me; their jauntiness and his yearning look, and I knew that I had to learn more about the secret meaning underneath this encounter.

Because as I, too, watched them stride down the road, the Earth itself seemed to lose some of its terrible solidity and began to shift and move and dance in a cockeyed rhythm.

So from that moment I embarked on an impossible journey of penetration into a world where I did not belong—a study of the viewpoint of a crowd of teen-age boys. This was not easy.

Even though I had three teen-age sons of my own at home, I knew that the teen-ager by himself at home with parents is one person. But when he is with a crowd of his fellows his personality blends into theirs, and out of this blending emerges something else—something special—a conglomerate individual; irreverent, omnipotent, happy, and wise.

But when the adult, hearing them in a heated discussion of bebop, long hair, politics, or sex, ventures into the same room, they become inarticulate and wait for him to return to his own generation.

So I tried guile. I invited groups of them on trips with me and a woman friend from time to time, and these laboratory excursions cost me more than money.

For instance, I walked once into the best hotel at Aspen, Colorado, leading five of them—one my son—and four of his friends

—and registered for all of us with what I thought was dignity. Only to turn and see one of them sidle up to the room clerk.

"Would you be good enough to keep this in the hotel safe for me, my good man?" His voice was stern as he laid an empty half grapefruit rind on the register and then walked across the lobby, which was full of visiting intellectuals, with a knock-kneed tremor.

The clerk's eyes traveled carefully over the register, over my luggage and my clothes.

"Are these boys ALL with you, Mrs. Chase?" Then he looked at the grapefruit.

Something told me I could never explain it, so silently I picked up the grapefruit, dropped it into my purse, and followed two bellboys upstairs to the suite.

"This is the clothes closet, Madam," said one of the bellboys, as he opened the closet door with a flourish.

Out of the closet stepped three of the boys in great indignation. They frowned at him.

"No privacy, no privacy at all. Call the manager."

But the manager was already at the door to see me.

"Mrs. Chase, the boys you have with you will not be permitted in the dining room in the blue jeans they are wearing. They must wear proper suits, neckties, and shirts."

This the boys refused to do and they dined at a hamburger place around the corner, while my woman friend and I chatted in a polite twosome in little dinner dresses over the fine French cuisine in the elegant little Victorian dining room. At the main table near by sat a group of college professors and Mr. Justice Black, all in Aspen to take part in a panel discussion that evening at the old opera house.

Suddenly we looked up to see the boys in blue jeans marching toward us carrying hamburgers in oiled papers. They laid them on the white linen cloth.

"We bit off more than we could chew—so we brought you some—eat hearty, ladies."

With the eyes of the French waiters hard upon us and telling ourselves we didn't care, we put the hamburgers into our evening bags and made as dignified an exit as two women might make out of a burning building.

But later that same evening, at the opera house where the subject of the panel discussion was "Merits of a Benign Dictatorship," the boys sat and listened with absorption.

Afterward on the street outside we were relieved as well as embarrassed when they fell into a wrestling match. Their pointed penetrating questions about the lecture had been too discerning for us to answer—questions about this world we were leaving to them.

Another time with a friend, I took another son and four of his friends to the Broadmoor Hotel in Colorado Springs where they could ride, swim, and hike.

This group agreed to the neckties and shirts for the dining room. But while out walking over the grounds before dinner, my friend and I were stopped by a strange sight.

This group of five stood on the children's playgrounds. Each boy was eighteen or a few months over and each carried a draft registration card in his pocket. But they were grouped around a piece of playground equipment, an iron pole with metal chains and rings. They were quietly watching a little girl of about seven years who had the gadget to herself and was swinging around and around on it.

The boys looked as though they had been waiting for it quite a while and the little girl looked as though she would swing on it forever. Finally the boys began to converse in a low, casual tone.

"Wasn't that a terrible accident this afternoon on that thing with that poor little girl," one inquired innocently.

"Bloodiest sight I ever saw," another answered. "That's a plenty dangerous ring."

The little girl was made of stern stuff. She ignored all of it until her mother called her.

At this I saw all five of them, each six feet tall, pounce with a leap and a great roar onto the rings and go swinging around dragging their feet in the dust, laughing and yelling like Indians.

Always on returning from these excursions—and I never knew when they were acquired—I would find in the turtle back of my car, metal signs: "Mezzanine, this way," "Half mile to ski lift," and "This pool for use of hotel guests only."

They would bring them to our house and carefully arrange these signs, sometimes at the bottom of trees in our garden or on the roof of the summer house.

And it wasn't until much, much later when I saw some of these same boys again, after they had grown out of their teens and into responsibility, that I was able to answer certain of the questions about them which had haunted me.

But in the meantime, while I was following them or bribing them to follow me, I noticed that they collected a strange and varied tribute from other age groups as they wandered in crowds up and down streets, through department stores and restaurants.

For instance, the sight of them arouses adoration in the eyes of all small boys and all grandmothers; scorn and resentment from certain middle-aged men; and a deep yearning from almost all old, old men.

It is a Hallowe'en world they live in for a little while and their light heartedness comes, I believe, from the fact that as they stand on the top of a hill, as it were, and look at the Earth beneath, they do not quite believe in it; so they give off with a Bronx cheer and with an index finger draw crazy circles in the sky—blending skyscrapers and grapefruit rinds, bankers and bebop in a Daliesque signature. They own nothing of it and so they own it all.

And I think now that the old banker looked at them that morning because he was nearing the end of it and beginning to doubt a lot of it himself.

The bond between them was a kind of childish incredulity and they had passed like warriors to and from a battlefield of illusion.

Time takes boys such as these step by step into the valley of adulthood and then they become a little afraid, responsible, ambitious, and even greedy—just like all the rest of us.

But there is always another group of them silhouetted against the sky, and for myself—I think it is the most wonderful sight in the whole world.

MARY CHASE

Denver, Colorado
1953

Cast of Characters

WILL McELROY (MAC)	*A lower classman*
DAVE GIBBS	*A lower classman*
MORGAN OLSON (DINK)	*An upper classman*
LEONARD CARNEY (LEN)	*An upper classman*
ARTHUR BEAUMONT (BEAU)	*An upper classman*
MARVIN GRINER (TUB)	*An upper classman*
GEORGE FRIEDELHAUSER (FUDGE)	*An upper classman*
BUFORD WELDY (WORMY)	*An upper classman*
RUTH WELDY	*His mother*
SELMA CANTRICK	*Her friend*
VERNON KINSWOOD	*A family friend*
ENID LACEY	*Mrs. Weldy's friend*
JEAN CANTRICK	*Selma Cantrick's daughter*
A.J. WITNICK	*Hotel Manager*
EDDIE	*A bellboy*
HELEN	*A waitress*
WOLF	*A wolf*

Policemen, hotel guests, porters.

The entire action of the play takes place in one day in a city in the Far West in the present.

Scenes

ACT ONE

A street; The Shamrock; Mrs. Weldy's home; the lobby of the Barclay Hotel.

ACT TWO

Mrs. Lacey's apartment; a street; Mrs. Weldy's home; The Shamrock.

✳   ✳   ✳

On the night of 16 October 1952, Irving L. Jacobs presented the Guthrie McClintic Production of *Bernardine* at the Playhouse Theatre, New York City.

PROLOGUE

Just before the curtain rise.

The orchestra rises in the pit and goes away. The buzzing in the audience subsides. The house lights dim. A pin spotlight moves across the thick red velvet curtain and picks out a young man stepping from behind the curtain to face the audience. He is in the uniform of the United States Air Force. He smiles. He says:

"Good evening, folks. My name is Arthur Beaumont. I'm a lieutenant in the Air Force—but I used to be a King.

"There are quite a few of us retired Kings flying these days. But often in the service clubs and around we get together and talk about our lost kingdoms; high-school days in the old home town—a Hallowe'en world that is—with its own set of rulers, values, dreams, and a cockeyed edge to laughter.

"Here no adult can enter fully—ever.

"The fellows I knew at the Shamrock—that's a three-two beer place, four blocks from the high school—they're all gone now. Where? It doesn't matter because, like me, they've grown up and stepped into an adult world.

"But I'd like to show you one day a couple of years ago, in the Kingdom of that Hallowe'en world, what we did there, what we said and how we felt about each other—in particular—a kid named Wormy Weldy.

"Well—shall we take a look?"

He disappears and the curtain slowly rises.

Act I

TIME: *Saturday afternoon of a spring day.*

SCENE: *The curtain rises and we are looking at four teen-age boys standing on a city street. At stage left is the entrance of a drugstore. At stage right the entrance to an office building. In the distance, painted on the backdrop, rise the chimneys and bell tower of a large high-school building.*

The two boys standing at stage left wear blue jeans and white shirts, the tails hanging outside; flat hats, tightly rolled into a pancake shape, the brims stuck with colored feathers. One of these boys, GIBBS, *has his leg thrown over a bicycle. These boys are about sixteen years old.*

At stage right stand two older boys, about eighteen. They wear no hats. They wear T shirts and suede jackets with the letter H emblazoned on the backs in bright-colored paint. Their manner toward the younger boys is patronizing. The manner of the younger boys toward them is deferential.

CARNEY. (*One of the older boys speaks first. He is handsome but slight of build. As he speaks he makes a move up the street. He addresses his companion, a boy with a crew cut.*) Come on, Olson, we'll be shovin' off. (OLSON *who walks with a slight limp moves after him.*)

MC ELROY. (*One of the younger boys whispers in a low tone to his pal. He has a sensitive, alert face.*) Let's go with 'em, Gibbs. (*He follows the older boys across the stage. He tries to make his voice and manner casual.*) Hey—where you guys shovin' to?

CARNEY. (*He stops.*) Down to the back room of the Shamrock.

CARNEY

OLSON. (*Grandly.*) We're supposed to meet Beaumont and them.

MC ELROY. (*This impresses him.*) Beaumont and them! On the level?

OLSON. Yup!

MAC. (*Dreamily.*) Beaumont is in my gym class at school. He speaks to me.

GIBBS. (*He is a heavy-set boy with sandy hair and freckles. He inches forward on the bike.*) Beaumont! My Dad—I mean—my old man knows his old man.

CARNEY. (*Sternly.*) Listen, Gibbs, that don't necessarily get anybody in solid with a guy just because his old man knows their old man.

OLSON. Beaumont picks his own friends. He has his own ideas. Let's shove, Carney.

MAC. (*Still following them.*) How about Gibbs and me stringin' along down there with you guys? (OLSON *and* CARNEY *exchange a weighty glance.*)

OLSON. I don't know how Beau and Tub and them would take that. What do you think, Carney?

CARNEY. (*Carefully looking at the younger boys.*) Frankly, I'm worried. Remember Pritchard and Wilson? They got tossed out on their ear. We lost, Olson, a certain amount of prestige.

[6]

MAC. (*With a sneer.*) Pritchard and Wilson! No wonder.

GIBBS. McElroy has three bucks on him and my Dad—my old man is gettin' me a '41 Plymouth next month. (OLSON *and* CARNEY *again exchange a weighty glance at this information. They give* GIBBS *closer scrutiny. He sees their hesitancy and moves closer.*) Oh boy! Did me and Mac have a big time last night! We sneaked his old man's car and picked up a couple of babes!

CARNEY. (*With contempt.*) First time I did that I was fourteen years old.

GIBBS. Boy, did we make time with those babes! I had my arm around one of them for a block and a half. Didn't we have a big time last night, Mac? (*He nudges* MAC *to bear him out.*)

MAC. (*Coldly, pulling away from* GIBBS.) Last night? I forgot last night awready. (CARNEY *and* OLSON *note* MAC'S *nonchalance with approval. With his last remark he has made a definite impression and a promise of inner riches.*)

CARNEY. (*Goes to him and lays a hand on his shoulder.*) You might be O.K., Mac—yup—you just might. Gibbs—

GIBBS. (*Eagerly.*) Yeah?

CARNEY. (*His face serious.*) Never slap it down like that. If you see a chance to slide it in—slide it in but otherwise "didn't we make time with those babes last night"—don't do it. It sounds boastful. It sounds—

OLSON. Immature.

CARNEY. Yeah! You worry me, Gibbs. You've got an awful tendency to be an awful square.

MAC

GIBBS. (*He is horrified.*) A square! Me? A square? What are you talkin' about?

CARNEY. I'm afraid you'll never make the grade as a smooth operator or a big wheel. What do you think, Dink, could he go along as a husk?

OLSON. (*With the air of an expert.*) Let go of your kiddie car and step out here a minute, boy. Let's look at you. (GIBBS *gives the bike to* MAC *to steady for him. He steps briskly over to the two older boys who now begin to feel his arms and shoulders.*)

CARNEY. He packs a lot of weight and muscle. Of course, I've never seen him in a sluggin' match.

MAC. He's not bad, this boy.

OLSON

CARNEY. He's a husk all right, but a husk can be an awful chicken too. But a husk who's not afraid to fight—well—that's an ugh-me-fix. (*He pounds chest and speaks Indian fashion as he says "ugh-me-fix" and clenches fists.*) An ugh-me-fix is a great help to the gang if there's any trouble at a dance or at a hamburger place after a dance. Yup—if he's got any nerve he can aim for an ugh-me-fix. Think you'd like to aim for an ugh-me-fix, Gibbs?

OLSON. Because you are not the big wheel type—definitely not.

CARNEY. Never in the world.

OLSON. Gibbs, you don't have the—what is it he don't have, Carney? I know he don't have it, but I don't know if I can tell why.

GIBBS. (*Sullenly.*) What's Beaumont got that I haven't got—except he's a little older. (*All the boys laugh loudly.*)

MAC. (*He regards his friend ruefully. It had never occurred to him before, but maybe* GIBBS *is a bit square.*) You're talkin' outta turn right now, Gibbs.

[8]

GIBBS. Why? I'm only askin' a question.

CARNEY. (*Sadly.*) There's some questions, Gibbs, you never ask. You know the answer awready and if you don't—you're a square. Beaumont! (*Here he steps forward, hands in pockets and his eyes glow with admiration.*) Beaumont has got everything! He's got—

OLSON. Plenty of savvy. He's smooth and he's hep and he's with it all the way.

CARNEY. Gets by big with women. He can hold his liquor. Never makes a bum crack at the wrong time. And style—that's it— Beaumont stinks with style.

OLSON. And can you imagine Beaumont ever askin' anybody what somebody had that he didn't have?

CARNEY. That's because Beaumont KNOWS he's got everything.

GIBBS. My old man is playin' golf today with Beaumont's old man so what are you guys givin' me about Beaumont?

OLSON. But listen, Gibbs—it's not your old man that's yappin' to go with us down to the Shamrock!

MAC. (*Desperately.*) Look—do we go with you guys—or don't we?

CARNEY. That's up to Gibbs. If he sees the situation and takes a little advice he might just make the grade with the gang. Give up the big wheel stuff, Gibbs. Keep in trim and try to go along as an ugh-me-fix. Of course, you don't get the choice babes, but you're in the crowd, boy, you're in the crowd.

GIBBS. (*Despite a warning look from MAC.*) You guys are full of a lot of chatter and I'm not sayin' if I'm buyin' it or if I'm not buyin' it. I know I couldn't be a big operator on this bicycle but I told you my old man is gettin' me a '41 Plymouth next month, so I don't know if you guys have sold me anything or if you haven't sold me anything.

MAC. (*To* CARNEY *and* OLSON.) So what gives?

CARNEY. (*Still doubtful.*) What do you think, Olson?

OLSON. (*His eyes on* MAC.) We'll take a chance on 'em. But re-member, when we get down to the Shamrock—no bum cracks —see!

GIBBS. We heard you! We heard you!

CARNEY. Okay, Gibbs—just get with it—get with it. (*The two older boys move up the street.* MAC *hurries after them, his face jubilant.* GIBBS *is last, puffing as he tries to run and haul the bicycle.*)

BLACKOUT

TIME: *A few minutes later.*

SCENE: *The back room of the Shamrock—a three-two beer parlor, four blocks from the high school.*

This is a shabby spot. There is no reason apparent to the eye why it has been the favorite "hang out" for years of the upper classmen at nearby Holbrook Hi. But favorite "hang out" it is for those intangible reasons which will cause boys to pass up neat, gaily painted, happy, sunny rooms, and disappear into shabby, dull, musty, dusty places like this. Tradesmen and shopkeepers have always puzzled over this problem, and always will. The lure of such a spot defies all accountants and business experts. It gets the "play" for some mysterious reason. The crowd goes there. Why? No one knows.

Perhaps the boys are soothed by the spirits and memories of hundreds of other boys who have loved it and have come here to settle those deep and desperate problems of the heart and mind not solved in the classrooms.

The walls are covered with initials, telephone numbers, crude drawings of bathing girls, football scores, and an outdated calendar with the picture of a jet plane.

The tables are old and rickety, the brown wooden booths sagging and creaky. They have endured years of wrestling, overcrowding. The telephone booth against the wall at stage left has a hinge off the door. The telephone book on a high wooden stand near by is torn and scribbled.

A light from the outside street pours through a green glass window high on the wall. A jukebox stands under it.

As the lights go up, this jukebox is playing a piece of modern music with a trumpet solo. On stage are three boys—two standing, one seated at the table, his head in his hands. They are listening intently.

One boy at left, FUDGE FRIEDELHAUSER, *a husky boy with a naïve expression is the gang "husk." He stands with one foot on a chair. Leaning against the wall across from him is* MARVIN (TUB) GRINER. GRINER *is muscular, shrewd-eyed. His shrewd eyes show that he is "hep" and his jaw denotes physical courage. Girls find him attractive. He is the prime "wolf" of the gang.*

Seated at the table is ART BEAUMONT, *the gang leader.* BEAUMONT'S *face is a combination of fierceness and sensitivity. He is tall and lean. His manner is mocking and he assumes, to mask himself, a cloak-and-dagger manner of bravado, and yet his moods change like lightning. His smile is rare but sweet.*

TUB. (*Indicating the jukebox with a jerk of his thumb.*) He doesn't blow it like he means it.

FUDGE. You're not listening—he means it.

TUB. (*Shakes his head as he listens to another note of the trumpet.*) If he means it—he doesn't make it.

BEAUMONT. (*He hasn't heard them—his expression rapt.*) Dig it—dig that sound —that cool, cool sound. (*The other*

TUB

[12]

boys are impressed with BEAUMONT's *approval of the trumpet player. They wait and listen.*)

TUB. (*Hesitantly—first glancing at* BEAUMONT.) You sure that's Martiniz?

FUDGE. (*He grins happily.*) That's Martiniz.

TUB. Oh, he stinks anymore. He used to be good but he stinks now. Bevans is hot now.

FUDGE. Bevans is plenty hot.

BEAUMONT. (*He rises and walks across the stage, his hands in his pockets.*) Martiniz! He can no longer run the distance, but he can still hurt you. (*Enter* CARNEY *and* OLSON.)

FUDGE

CARNEY. Hi, Beau, Tub, Fudge.

BEAUMONT. (*His eyes gleam with a mocking light but fond as he looks at them. He makes his expression comically fierce. He gives a wave of the hand, moving each finger as though he were playing the piano in mid-air. There is a weary elegance in this gesture. Behind his back the other boys practice it at home trying to imitate him.*) Greetings—men!

TUB. Where you been? We got problems.

OLSON. Messin' around. Say—we brought a couple of fellows with us.

CARNEY. A couple of plenty sharp boys.

BEAUMONT. (*Languidly.*) Who?

OLSON. Will McElroy and Dave Gibbs.

[13]

FUDGE. (*Moving to* BEAUMONT.) They're a couple of twinks. I've seen them.

TUB. (*He sneers as he moves toward* BEAUMONT.) Sharp boys! That Gibbs is still ridin' a bicycle.

OLSON. Listen—his old man is gettin' him a '41 Plymouth next month.

TUB. (*To* BEAUMONT.) Why should we mess around with that young stuff?

OLSON. McElroy looks old. He's sixteen but he could pass for eighteen. You'll like him, Beau. You'll be callin' him Fofo.

BEAU

CARNEY. What about it, Beau?

BEAUMONT. (*Still languid.*) We can always throw them out—so let them in.

CARNEY. (*Now runs to the entrance and bawls out loudly.*) Hey, you creeps—haul it on in here! (MC ELROY *and* GIBBS *now enter. They try to appear nonchalant and hide their great eagerness and excitement. But they are like bear cubs trying to walk on two legs.* MC ELROY *looks around warily. He will feel his way. But* GIBBS *has already decided on the swaggering, bold "You guys have nothing on me" approach.* CARNEY *steps forward and stands beside them to do the honors. He moves them as he makes the introductions as though he were pushing a hand merry-go-round.*) Guess maybe you guys might know these guys. Dave Gibbs and Will McElroy, Art Beaumont, Tub Griner, and Fudge Friedelhauser—Fudge Friedelhauser, Tub Griner, and Art Beaumont, Will McElroy and Dave Gibbs.

BEAUMONT. (*He rises, walks around them, goes over to the wall, and leans against it.*) Greetings—men! (*He now makes the*

[14]

same finger-waving movement. TUB *and* FUDGE *both mumble a weak "Hi."*)

GIBBS. (*To their amazement has the temerity to walk directly over to* BEAUMONT.) My Dad plays golf with your Dad, Beaumont.

BEAUMONT. (*Coolly with a raised eyebrow.*) Oh!

GIBBS. (*Blissfully unaware of his mistake—in this familiarity.*) My Dad says your Dad is the best engineer in the whole state.

BEAUMONT. (*With sarcasm.*) Well—well—well!

GIBBS. He says not another man could have built that Mt. Secrist Tunnel with nature against him.

BEAUMONT. (*Pretending to yawn.*) I barely—(*He flicks the ash off a cigarette*) know the man.

GIBBS. (*He is puzzled but not discouraged. He walks over to* TUB GRINER.) I've seen you around, Griner. You've got a '46 Nash.

TUB. (*Moves away from him.*) 'Forty-eight. And that used to be a Nash but it's not a Nash anymore.

GIBBS. (*But* GIBBS, *although wilting, is not squelched.* MC ELROY *watches him and suffers.* GIBBS *goes up to* FUDGE *with a heartiness.*) Hi, Friedelhauser! I've seen you play football. You're not bad, boy.

FUDGE. And I'm not Friedelhauser either. (*He moves away.*)

BEAUMONT. (*Lays a fond arm across* FUDGE's *shoulder and takes on the deep gruff tone of a big-time business official.*) This man's name is Bidnut—Fofo Bidnut. He is a traveling man— hard candies. How is business, Mr. Bidnut—little slow—eh— little slow?

GIBBS. (*Puzzled.*) But I've seen him play—

MAC. (*He is sure now that* GIBBS *has ruined both of their chances.*

[15]

He pulls at his sleeve and says fiercely) Skip it. Shut up. (*He turns to* BEAUMONT.) Okay if we sit down, Beaumont? (*He starts to lower himself to the floor.* GIBBS *has already sat down.*)

BEAUMONT. (*In sudden alarm.*) Look out for that floor—she tips.

GIBBS. (*Jumping up.*) She—what?

MAC. (*Pulling him down.*) Shut up. Sit down. (MC ELROY, *who is watching like a cat, offers* GIBBS *a cigarette with a casual air. They both light up as the older boys study them. There is a moment of silence.*)

GIBBS. (*He will not be quiet.*) This is a pretty nice spot here. But the Rancho—that's the real spot. Ever been to the Rancho, Beaumont?

TUB. Been to it—he just sold it.

CARNEY. (*Anxious to get the limelight off* GIBBS.) What happened to you last night, Beau?

OLSON. We came by and you weren't here. Did you have a date?

BEAUMONT. Last night? (*Such a long time ago. He finally remembers.*) Oh—yes, yes—I had a date. This friend from out of town she drove in from Idaho in her '52 Cad convertible.

GIBBS. (*He inches forward. His eyes are bugged out.*) Saaay!

BEAUMONT. (*In confidential tone.*) You know something, Griner? She may take that offer from Hollywood after all. They have been driving the little thing nuts.

TUB. (*He plays up.*) Well—now—

BEAUMONT. (*Dreamily.*) But it's just like I told her. You don't need them, sugar. You've got me. And she smiled as I pried her arms from around my neck. I had to pry and pry and pry. She would not let go—the little tiger!

GIBBS. Wow!

[16]

BEAUMONT. (*Throwing his head forward—putting one hand to the back of his neck.*) Take a look there, fellows. She leave any marks? (*While* GIBBS *and* MC ELROY *stare, the gang leaps forward and gazes with mock solemnity at* BEAUMONT's *neck. They give forth a chorus of* "Oooh—ahh—look at that—jeepers.")

OLSON. (*In shocked tone.*) You better get a doctor to take a look at that, Beaumont!

GIBBS. (*This is indeed the world he belongs in—he thinks.*) Saaay —who is this babe?

BEAUMONT. Tell him, Class.

BOYS. Bernardine—Bernardine Crud!

MAC. Bernardine Crud—where does she go to school?

BEAUMONT. (*Turns to the two younger boys.*) School! She's through school. She's lived. (*He fools with his jacket dreamily.*) She's a little older—little beat up looking but not too much. Just misty and dreamy. Her hair is blonde about so long—

GIBBS. Oh boy!

MAC. What do you know!

BEAUMONT. You couldn't miss her. When she walks down the street, her eyes flash a message—live on, boy, dream on. I'm waiting for you. But as for actual conversation she knows only one word.

MAC. Only one word—what's that?

BEAUMONT. (*Shyly dropping his head.*) The word is—yes.

TUB. (*With feeling.*) That's a good word.

GIBBS. Jeepers—where does this babe live?

BEAUMONT. Now that's an interesting question. She lives in a little town in the mountains of Idaho, on the banks of Itching River —a place called Sneaky Falls.

[17]

GIBBS. (*He takes out notebook and pencil.*) Sneaky Falls?

BEAUMONT. It's away up in the mountains. Terrible roads—busses not running. Of course, you could make it in a super jet. (*Walks languidly over to the wall and faces* GIBBS.) You've heard of it, of course.

GIBBS. (*Brightly.*) Oh, sure, sure. (*The other boys exchange an amused glance with* BEAU.)

MAC. I never did. (BEAU'S *eyes linger now on* MC ELROY *with interest, but he gazes sternly at* GIBBS, *although his voice is dangerously gentle.*) You have, Gibbs?

GIBBS. Yeah, seems to me we passed through there last summer on our way home from Winnemucca.

BEAUMONT. Well, well—well—very, very interesting. (*Turns now as* HELEN, *a waitress about thirty with dyed red hair and spotted apron, comes in with pad and pencil.*) Greetings, Helen—what about a round of beer here?

HELEN. Okay— (*Sees the younger boys. Her lips clamp. She walks to them.*) What's YOUR order?

GIBBS. Two beers, light on the head.

HELEN. I said—what's your order?

GIBBS. Just gave you the order.

HELEN. Yeah? Let's see your draft cards.

MAC. (*Slaps at his pockets. But he determines to bluff.*) Well— what did I do with that thing? Must have left it in my other suit.

HELEN. Your snow suit?

GIBBS. Say—listen you!

MAC. Aw, what's the difference? We'll get one after a while.

[18]

HELEN. I'll get my old-age pension after a while too. (*Goes angrily to the older boys.*) Don't try to pull this on me! Do you want the old man to lose his license? Just because he lets you kids with draft cards have a glass of three-two in here don't try to drag in a kindergarten. (*Looks at* MAC *and* GIBBS.) Pepsi-Cola—cola cola— (*She exits quickly.*)

MAC. Two cokes. The deal stinks.

BEAUMONT. McElroy—come over here.

MAC. (*He starts to rise with alacrity and then stops. His eyes meet* BEAUMONT'S *in a test of character. He slowly drops back down. He speaks and his eyes and gaze are steady.*) Why should I?

BEAUMONT. (*Gazes at him silently—approvingly. Then he smiles suddenly—a gentle, tender smile. The others boys are looking at* MAC *with the same silent approval.* MAC *doesn't realize it yet but he has passed a milestone in his life. The boys are beginning to suspect that he may be a "hep" character—eager to make the gang but not willing to give everything to do it. When* BEAUMONT *speaks his voice is soft.*) No reason at all, Mac—none at all.

MAC. Okay.

BEAUMONT. You're all right, Mac. Yup—you may be perfectly all right.

GIBBS. (*Feeling this is the time to wade in with both feet and establish himself and* MAC *as big men.*) Me and Mac sure had a time last night—didn't we, Mac?

MAC. Shh—shut up!

GIBBS. Mac swiped his old man's car and we picked up a couple of babes. Boy—we made pretty good time with those babes—eh, Mac?

BEAUMONT. (*Swiftly turning to* MAC.) Eh, Mac?

[19]

MAC. (*With a look of disgust at* GIBBS.) I forget. (BEAU *looks at the other boys over* MAC's *head and makes an approving circle in the air with his thumb and forefinger. They nod in agreement.*)

TUB. (*With a stern voice gives his attention to* GIBBS.) You knew these girls, of course?

GIBBS. (*Happily.*) Knew 'em? Of course not. We picked 'em up.

TUB. (*With an air of regret makes a disapproving clucking sound with his tongue. He sighs.*) Hear that, Beaumont?

BEAUMONT. (*Covering his face with his hands.*) I wish I hadn't.

TUB. You were taking an awful chance, Gibbs, taking strange tomatoes into your car.

GIBBS. (*Throwing one leg over the other.*) Chance? It was them that was taking the chance—eh, Mac?

BEAUMONT. Gibbs, you are the type of character who gives our school a bad name.

FUDGE. Weldy's old lady thinks it's us—but it's you.

GIBBS. Hey! What is this? With the reputations you guys have got for smooth operators and big wheels—what is this?

BEAUMONT. (*Ignores* GIBBS—*goes to* MAC.) McElroy—tell us the story of your life in two words—

MAC. Two words—gosh—

BEAUMONT. Gibbs could do it in two words—I stink—beat it— Gibbs—

GIBBS. What?

FUDGE. Wanta get hurt—blow—

GIBBS. Comin', Mac—

[20]

MAC. I don't know yet—

GIBBS. All right for you, Mac—next time you—

TUB. Beat it—(*With a reproachful glance at* MAC, GIBBS *goes quickly.*)

BEAUMONT. Two words, Mac—like this—Fudge—

FUDGE. I slug—

BEAUMONT. Carney—

CARNEY. I scheme—

OLSON. I bull—

BEAUMONT. Tub—better use the nice word—tomorrow's Sunday.

TUB. I conquer.

BEAUMONT. And I laugh— (*He gives a mocking, horrible, and yet comic laugh.*) Now you, Mac—

MAC. (*Bewildered.*) I—I—wonder! (*The boys all laugh.*)

BEAUMONT. (*Grabs his hand eagerly.*) You're all right, Mac. Fellows, I want you to meet Mr. Bidnut of Sneaky Falls, Idaho— Mr. Bidnut—Mr. Bidnut—Mr. Bidnut—Mr. Bidnut— (*They all shake* MAC's *hand eagerly. He is in. His face is jubilant.*)

BEAUMONT. Say—we're missing one—where is I maul—where is Weldy?

MAC. (*The mention of this name has a staggering effect on him.*) Weldy—you don't mean Wormy Weldy? Is he part of this gang?

BEAUMONT. (*Wheels around and looks at him fiercely.*) And what's wrong with that?

MAC. He's a wild man. (BEAUMONT *nods, still studying him.*)

Weldy—he got expelled from Winston Hi—twice before he came to Holbrook!

TUB. Twice—three times! (BEAUMONT's *eyes are still fastened on* MAC's *face. His gaze is intense and yet curiously detached and amused. He now holds up three fingers.*)

MAC. Weldy—he's the guy who put a stick of dynamite into the drain pipe at the gym last year.

CARNEY. He put in two sticks—that was all he had. (BEAUMONT *holds up two fingers, still gazing at* MAC.)

FUDGE. He's changed though—he don't care a thing about dynamite anymore.

OLSON. He's changed—to dames and has he gone crazy!

BEAUMONT. (*Softly.*) And he is a very good friend of ours.

MAC. Well, I guess he's got plenty of nerve. I guess there's nothing he's afraid of. (*All the boys laugh loudly.*)

BEAUMONT. Oh yes there is—his old lady.

CARNEY. She's trying to be a companion to him. She thinks of him as a delicate flower and keeps going over him with a garden rake.

TUB. He called on the telephone this morning and said he was about to launch a one-man mutiny against her but he hasn't been able to sneak out of the house to get it launched.

MAC. Weldy! (*He moves—shaking his head.*) Gee—you oughta hear my old lady talk about him!

BEAUMONT. And you ought to hear Weldy's old lady talk about us!

MAC. (*This is a bitter moment. He has made the grade but the price is too high. He moves toward the door. He stops. His voice is wistful.*) It was great seeing you guys—great—great!

BEAUMONT. Yes it was, Mac— It was tender. It was real. (MAC *runs out. The boys all look at* MAC's *fleeing figure and shrug at each other.*)

CARNEY. Huh! It was tender. It was real. And it was WELDY! (*There is the ringing of the telephone.* CARNEY *runs to answer it. He holds the receiver, turns grinning to the boys.*)

CARNEY. (*In the tone of the baby bear in "Goldilocks."*) —and here he is now! (*He hands the telephone to* BEAUMONT.)

BLACKOUT

ACT ONE

SCENE 3

TIME: *Immediately following scene two.*

SCENE: *The living room of the Weldy home.*

This is a tastefully furnished room with the predominating colors of plum and soft yellow. An archway, center stage back, leads into a hall which runs left and right. There is a deep bay window beyond the arch. This window, curtained with white ruffles, shows in the distance the spires of a church across a park.

There are a few choice pieces of Victorian furniture, chairs, tables, and a love seat, which blend pleasantly with modern reproductions of French provincial and Chippendale.

Everything in this room is dainty, feminine, and tasteful— that is, everything but BUFORD WELDY, *called* WORMY *by his friends.*

He is a muscular, blond boy with a cleft in his strong chin, and is standing now at the telephone at stage left. He is wearing a neat outfit for a Saturday afternoon; slacks, white shirt, necktie, and sports jacket. He always leaves his home dressed this way. A block away from the house, however, he will pull off the necktie, jam it into his pocket, rumple his hair, let his shirt tail hang out over the slacks, and carry his jacket over his arm.

WORMY. (*His tone is severe.*) Beaumont, I don't know why you guys even bother to call me. You must be crazy. I got no time

[25]

to fool around with you. I'm loaded with homework. Think I wanta flunk? Nope, I don't care what you got planned—count me out. (*He hangs up the phone and stands waiting.*) (*Enter* RUTH WELDY. *She has been listening in the hallway. Her face is beaming with pleasure.* RUTH WELDY *is a small woman, chic, neatly groomed, about forty-three years of age. Her voice and manner are crisp and sure, full of authority. Known to her friends as a "strong character," she has always known the security of a good income and a well-established social position in her home town. Self-doubt she would regard as a weakness. Behind her now walks a neatly dressed boy, carrying a raincoat. This is* VERNON KINSWOOD.)

RUTH. Buford—here's Vernon!

WORMY. (*Not looking up.*) Hi, slob!

KINSWOOD. Same old Wormy! Hi, Wormy.

RUTH. Now, boys, boys! Buford, don't speak to Vernon like that.

VERNON. (*Smiling at her.*) Wormy doesn't bother me none, Mrs. Weldy. He's always crackin' off.

RUTH. And Vernon, please, please don't call him by that awful nickname. I despise it. His name is Buford. Tell him the news, dear.

WORMY

WORMY. What news?

RUTH. What news? Listen to you! Vernon, we have an addition to the family. I bought a dog yesterday.

WORMY. (*With great bitterness as he looks out the window.*) Yeah—she bought me a dog.

[26]

RUTH. A darling little dachshund. I'm ashamed I haven't done it before. Buford wanted one for years but I was thinking of the garden. Every boy should have a dog.

WORMY. (*He gets an idea.*) Say—ah—he oughta have some exercise. Why don't me and Kinswood take him for a little walk?

RUTH. That's a fine idea. You and Vernon take him over to the park for half an hour.

KINSWOOD. (*He frowns.*) It's all right, but I did promise Mother I'd pick up some things for her at the store.

RUTH

WORMY. (*Now very warm to* KINSWOOD. *He walks quickly to him and slaps him on the back.*) We can do that while we're out, Kinswood. Easiest thing in the world. (*He starts to leave the room.*)

RUTH. (*Laying a fond hand on his arm. She stands close to him and runs her hand over his sleeve, petting him.*) I'm pretty proud of my boy this afternoon, Vernon.

KINSWOOD. (*Who could be proud of* WORMY?) Oh—how's that?

RUTH. That gang just called him and tried to get him to meet them and he certainly told them off. Said he had no time for them. I stood right here and heard him. You did, didn't you, dear?

WORMY. Oh—well—I— (*Shrugs lamely and stops. His tone has been deprecating; a kind of "oh, it was nothing really, nothing."*)

KINSWOOD. That bunch never did anybody any good. They're a bunch of low-life bums, flunkin' in everything, always thinking about girls.

WORMY. (*Forgetting where he is.*) Listen, Kinswood, Carney did better than you in every class.

[27]

RUTH. Leonard Carney did better than Vernon? I don't believe it.

WORMY. (*Brusquely—as he moves toward the door*.) Hey, Kinswood, get the lead out—let's go.

RUTH. (*She stops him. Her table of standards is upset. Boys of whom she approves are the boys who get the good grades. Boys of whom she disapproves always flunk*.) Just a minute! You mean to tell me Carney actually got better grades than Vernon?

KINSWOOD. (*Regretfully*.) Carney is a brain all right. And yet he never seems to crack a book. I can't quite figure him out.

RUTH. I can't imagine, in that case, what Hilda and Frank Carney are thinking of to allow him to associate with Arthur Beaumont and that Griner boy.

WORMY. (*Very impatient*.) You comin', Kinswood?

KINSWOOD. (*Fiercely*.) Look, your mother's talkin' to me, stupe.

RUTH. Buford! What is the matter with you? Vernon, you'll be amused at this. I'll just have to tell you this one.

KINSWOOD. (*He loves gossip*.) Yes, yes. (*He smiles*.)

KINSWOOD

RUTH. (*Confidentially*.) Mavis Griner was telling me the other day she was worried about Olson's influence on her son, Tub. How can she be so dense?

KINSWOOD. So she said that, did she? Well, well!

RUTH. Of course, it's Arthur Beaumont who is the real rotten apple there. My heart aches for his father. He thinks the sun rises and sets on that boy. He doesn't fool his mother though. Phil is such a brilliant man, you wonder how he could be so

[28]

dense about his own son. Poor man, he's due for a sad awakening one of these days.

KINSWOOD. Oh, they're all a bunch of bums. One is just as bad as the other.

WORMY. (*Heatedly, coming back into the room from the hall.*) Kinswood, you don't know a thing about those guys—not a thing.

RUTH. And neither does he, Vernon. He doesn't go around with them. He's only guessing.

WORMY. I know Carney beat the socks off him in that chemistry exam.

RUTH. Buford! (*She turns to* KINSWOOD.) Don't you mind, Vernon, those boys are so dissipated and so blasé they have nothing to look forward to. Your good time is coming.

WORMY. He's had it.

RUTH. Buford, that's quite enough. Vernon, you know I'm expecting you to stay to dinner and spend the night with Buford, if it's all right with your mother.

KINSWOOD. Thanks, Mrs. Weldy. I appreciate it and so does Mother.

WORMY. (*The time is passing.*) Come on, Kinswood—come on—come on. (WORMY *turns to go hurriedly from the room.* KINSWOOD *starts to follow.* WORMY'S *jaw drops as* SELMA CANTRICK *now enters from the hall.* SELMA CANTRICK *is a plump, good-natured woman, carrying an armload of packages.* WORMY'S *attitude at the sight of her is not only the usual bored attitude of a boy toward one of his mother's friends but he also acts shamefaced. He tries to get out quickly.*)

RUTH. Wait a minute, dear—say hello to Selma.

SELMA. (*Sitting down with a gasp of relief and spilling packages on the floor.*) Let me sit down. I'm dead. Hello, Buford.

WORMY. How do, Mrs. Cantrick. (*He tries to get out again.*)

SELMA. I haven't seen you around our house lately, Buford. Have you crossed my daughter off your list? (WORMY's *face becomes a beet red. He says nothing.*)

RUTH. Buford would never cross Jean off his list. Selma, have you met Vernon Kinswood—Mrs. Cantrick.

SELMA. How do you do— (*She turns away to* RUTH.) Ruth, could you—

RUTH. (*Oh, so fondly as she regards* VERNON.) You've probably heard Jean speak of him.

SELMA. (*She gives* KINSWOOD *another cursory glance. But she speaks slowly.*) No, I don't believe I have.

KINSWOOD. (*He wants to linger with them. He likes to talk to older women.*) I've heard my mother speak of you. I think she was on the Garden Club committee with you two years ago.

SELMA. Oh yes, of course. How is your mother? I hope she's well. (*At this question a look of despair comes over* WORMY's *face. He sits down now and crosses his arms over his chest.*)

KINSWOOD. She hasn't been exactly. She's had a sinus infection and that stirred up a lot of that old neuritis she had last year. She tries to do too much. And then she gets that old bronchitis of hers. But I'll tell her you asked for her.

SELMA. Please do. (*She is anxious to be alone with* RUTH.)

RUTH. I want her and your father to come over to dinner soon and then we'll all go to the concert. You and Buford, too. Better take your raincoat, dear. Vernon has his.

KINSWOOD. Mother made me take it. (*He looks at both women fondly.*) Guess you mothers are all alike—always worrying. (*He sighs with pleasure. The fact that mothers worry seems to him a wonderful thing.*)

SELMA. Ruth—I'm dying to tell you—

KINSWOOD. She likes concerts and that will be fine if only she doesn't get that dry hacking cough she gets when she has that sinus. Oh boy! When that happens is she down! Doc Granby won't let her stir out of the house. She had it all last winter. Sometimes I get tired of my Dad's cooking.

RUTH. (*In tone of dismissal.*) We'll try to cheer her up some night very soon. Don't be too long in the park, boys.

KINSWOOD. She was in bed last winter—from October—no—wait a minute here—from September until April. Couldn't seem to get ahead of the darned stuff.

SELMA. My—I do hope she's better very soon. (*The expression of despair on* WORMY's *face has deepened. He sighs. But* KINSWOOD's *face is radiant.*)

KINSWOOD. We thought it was her teeth—but no—she had them all out. My Dad said later it was a mistake. Too much of a shock to her system.

RUTH. What a shame! Selma, do you want to take your things upstairs?

KINSWOOD. Because she had to be on a special diet. Doc Benson, he's the specialist—he said she'd have to eat vegetable purée until he saw where he was at with it. He hasn't seen yet, though. But of course none of them will tell you anything.

SELMA. (*Thinking if she moves—maybe he will. She gets up and walks to the mirror.*) I do hope she's better very soon. Ruth—

KINSWOOD. (SELMA *is wrong.*) Oh, most of them are quacks! It's like my Dad says. They don't know how to do anything but make out their bills. You remember, Mrs. Weldy, last spring when she had that infected hair follicle?

RUTH. (*She sighs.*) Yes, yes—I do—Vernon.

KINSWOOD. (*To* SELMA.) We had three specialists and a couple of those high-powered machines but the worst of it was she couldn't seem to get any strength back.

RUTH. I think you boys better be getting started now.

WORMY. (*He doesn't rise.*) I think I'm too old to go now.

RUTH. I'd like for you both to have a cup of tea with us later.

WORMY. We can't come back 'til we leave. Haul it on out, Kinswood.

RUTH. You put the dog on the leash, dear. Vernon will be right along.

SELMA. I'll be upstairs, Ruth— (*She goes quickly with a last look of curiosity at* KINSWOOD.)

RUTH. (*Her tone is low. She draws* KINSWOOD *over to a corner.*) Vernon, you know how hard I'm working to keep Buford away from those boys. (*He nods very seriously.*) So Vernon, try to keep his mind on things like your rock collection and school, and now he has his dog. I wouldn't harm those boys for anything. I wouldn't injure any young person, I hope, but I just don't feel they're good for Buford. If the subject comes up, just put in a word about how you feel they're too advanced in some of their ideas—too sophisticated, and trying to show off; just rushing their development when they should be content to be schoolboys.

KINSWOOD. Sure, Mrs. Weldy. You bet I will.

RUTH. (*She makes her voice lower and pulls him farther into the corner.*) And don't let them get hold of him. If you should run into them simply say that you and Buford are busy with home-work this week end and have all of your plans made. Don't be rude or nasty—just be pleasant and keep right on going. They'll respect you all the more for it.

[32]

KINSWOOD. We sure will, Mrs. Weldy. Say—that's a mighty pretty dress.

RUTH. (*Gratefully.*) Oh, thank you, Vernon. How sweet of you! Whenever Buford is with you, I never worry about him at all. (*Runs to the window. She has seen* WORMY *in the yard.*) Buford, Buford—wait for Vernon—and get the dog, dear—get the dog!

BLACKOUT

TIME: *A half hour later.*

SCENE: *The back room of the Shamrock.*

CARNEY *is on the telephone.* WORMY *is seated center stage, his coat off, his necktie off, his hair rumpled. There is a half-empty glass of beer and an ashtray full of cigarette butts on the floor beside him.*

GRINER *is leafing through a telephone book copying numbers down on a piece of paper with a pencil.* BEAUMONT *leans across the table and studies a notebook.* OLSON *is writing names down on paper as* FUDGE *calls off old telephone numbers on the wall. There is an atmosphere of great concentration.*

As WORMY *listens to* CARNEY *his eyes grow eager with hope and then dull with disappointment.*

CARNEY. Okay, Louise, hang on a minute. (*He covers mouthpiece with his hand and addresses the boys, all of whom now look up.*) She says she will not take a blind date until I tell her who it's with. (*There is a loud groan from everyone.*)

TUB. If you tell her it's Weldy—we're cooked. Just tell her to take your word for it. (TUB *now returns to the telephone book.*)

CARNEY. (*Back into telephone.*) Take my word for it, Louise. This is a sharp boy. (*At this the boys all look at* WORMY *and*

sigh with weariness.) He's a good friend of mine. We'll all go out to the Rancho.

WORMY. (*Eagerly.*) Tell her I've got dough and I can borrow a '47 Buick.

CARNEY. Shh—Suppose we pick you up about eight. This boy drives a good car and he's got money, not peanuts. (*Covers phone again.*) She still wants to know who it is. (WORMY *sinks back into the chair.* TUB *walks to the telephone arrogantly.*)

TUB. (*Taking phone from* CARNEY.) Let me talk to her, Carney. (*He now settles his face into a wolfish expression, lowers his voice to a tone of wooing tenderness.*) How's my favorite wo-man? You don't think you are? Let's not be silly. Hum—um—hum. I've got a date tonight but you know who I wish it was with, don't you? Don't you? Hum?

OLSON. (*With admiration.*) That boy is smooth.

BEAUMONT. (*Grinning.*) He is really an operator.

WORMY. (*Wistfully.*) Maybe I oughta take some notes.

TUB. So I thought you and I could have a dance out there tonight and that's why I got this friend of mine for you. He's a swell boy—one of the best. What do you care about his name? We'll pick you up about eight, say.

WORMY. (*His eyes light up.*) They'll do anything for Tub.

CARNEY. Sounds like he's talked her into it.

TUB. I tell you you don't even know him. (*To boys, covering phone.*) She's stubborn. I'll have to take a chance and tell her. His name is Buford—um-hum. Yup—that's it. Weldy. (*He suddenly frowns. As he listens, he glares at* WORMY, *who squirms under his gaze and turns away.*) You don't say! I can't imagine it! That must have been one of his off nights. (*He hangs up and walks over to* WORMY.) She doesn't even live in this county. You get around, boy, you certainly get around. What did you do to her? (*He pulls up a chair and faces* WORMY.) Come on—let's have it.

CARNEY. That's at least twenty numbers we've called.

BEAUMONT. Wormy, I'm running out of names—even I.

WORMY. (*Avoiding* TUB'S *gaze.*) What about your date, Beau? She'll be able to get SOMEBODY? Didn't she say she could get SOMEBODY?

BEAUMONT. She said she'd try and call me back.

TUB. (*Still glaring at* WORMY.) Don't crawl. I asked you what you did to Louise Hostetter?

WORMY. I don't even know what she's talking about. Forget the drip and let's call somebody else.

BEAUMONT. Louise is not a drip. She's a good-type girl. What did you do to her, Fofo? They'll want to know in Sneaky Falls.

TUB. She claims he threw her in a creek.

CARNEY. You don't want a date. You want a wrestling match. Why are we knocking ourselves out, I wonder? Wormy, you're deceiving yourself. You don't know what a louse you really are.

WORMY. Listen—you guys are supposed to be my friends.

FUDGE. (*Walks up to* WORMY.) YOU threw Louise Hostetter in a creek!

BEAUMONT. Why did you throw that woman in a creek, Wormy —that's lousy technique!

FUDGE. Lousy! That's impossible! Louise Hostetter is five inches taller than you are and she outweighs you twenty-five pounds.

OLSON. Louise is a nice babe but she is also a big moose.

FUDGE. Weldy, I don't wanta know WHY. I want to know HOW!

WORMY. (*Desperately.*) Look, I tell you there wasn't a thing to it. I had a date with her once on a picnic but that was a long time ago. It's ancient history. Forget it. Carney, what about that little Sherman girl you used to date?

TUB. (*Still pursuing it.*) Louise says you were no more than intro-duced to her than you grabbed her and pulled her over into a clump of trees.

WORMY. (*Outraged.*) Listen to that! A clump of trees! That just shows you how they get things all mixed up. One tree it was—

[38]

one single tree. (*The telephone rings.* CARNEY *jumps to answer it. The boys all stop talking and listen.*)

CARNEY. Hello. What's that? Yeah. I'll find out. (*He turns to* WORMY.) Wormy, Ann Meggison can't go out tonight. Brownie wants to know if you'll take a date with Perkins?

TUB. The Reindeer!

WORMY. (*This is awfully hard to take.*) The Reindeer!

OLSON. Gee—Perkins does look like a Reindeer!

BEAUMONT. (*Very solemnly.*) Be fair, boys, be fair. Perkins does not look like a Reindeer—except in the face.

CARNEY. (*Into phone.*) Okay—if you can't do any better, he'll go with the Reindeer. (*Hangs up.*)

TUB. (*Moving his chair closer to* WORMY.) So?

WORMY. So what?

TUB. Why did you throw Louise Hostetter in that creek?

WORMY. But I told you. I just told you.

REAUMONT. You left us standing under a tree—one, single tree.

WORMY. Well, that night, it was a matter of my conscience. (HELEN, *the waitress, has come in now with a tray of beers. She leaves it on the table silently and walks out.* WORMY, *whose perusal of any woman is wholehearted and thorough, is watching her closely as she walks across the room. The fact that* HELEN *is faded, wispy-haired, and without glamour makes no difference. She is that mysterious creature—*WOMAN—*and if he studies long enough and looks hard enough—all mysteries may be revealed to him.* WORMY *is confident this moment is near at hand for him.*)

TUB. Conscience!

WORMY. (*Pulled back from* HELEN.) What? Oh! My old lady told me to be home by ten and it was eight-thirty when I got there, so I began to worry. I figured if I was going to make any time with this babe I'd better begin. My old lady never closes an eye 'til I get in. So—I reached over and put my arm around her. Right away she got heavy with me. So I said—"Look, babe, don't take this personally. I make these passes at everybody." She threw me in the creek. Well, the whole thing annoyed me and I climbed out and threw her in. She wasn't hurt any. There wasn't more than two inches of water in it. I tell you the woman means absolutely nothing to me—nothing.

TUB. (*Disgusted.*) If you'd told me this I'd never have stuck my neck out and asked for a blind date for you.

WORMY. I didn't mention it because there wasn't a thing to it. I'm not sore at her. She probably had a lot on her mind that night.

TUB. Your technique is stinking, Weldy.

WORMY. (*Indignant.*) What time do I get for technique? I get there at eight-thirty—ten miles out of town in the country—and have to be home by ten. Where's the time for technique? I don't get out often enough. (TUB *lets out a grunt of disgust and glares at* WORMY. *But* BEAUMONT, *who always arbitrates any difference of opinion, walks toward them.*)

BEAUMONT. He's right. But don't worry, Fofo—(*He pats* WORMY *on the back.*) Up in Sneaky Falls everything is different. Up there the mothers have to come to the boys for spending money and permission to leave the house. (*Now turns and faces an imaginary mother, placing arms akimbo.*) So, you say you're going downtown to lunch with women friends and you need five bucks? Who are these women? How do I know they're not bums? Go back upstairs. You're not leaving this house and take off that dirty old fox fur. (*The boys laugh but* BEAU *sits and leans back against the table, a dreamy expression crossing his face.*) Oh yes, when those busses start running again we'll all go up to Sneaky Falls and there, Wormy, a boy like you will get his revenge.

WORMY. (*Leans forward, his face caught in the same dream.*) Oh boy! Sneaky Falls, Idaho, on the shores of Itching River. And I hope up there, the girls are not jerks.

BEAUMONT. Every girl is Bernardine, and the word "no" is never spoken.

WORMY. Get those busses running—for God's sakes! (*All of the boys go into a dreamy slump about Sneaky Falls, which is broken by the ringing of the telephone.*)

CARNEY. (*He runs to answer it.*) Hello! Oh! It's for you, Beaumont.

BEAUMONT. (*Still relaxed and dreamy.*) Say I've gone to Sneaky Falls.

CARNEY. It's Johnson. You told her to call here about a date for Wormy.

BEAUMONT. (*Jumping up quickly.*) Johnson! (*As he picks up the phone he too gets his wolf voice ready and speaks into the instrument with a mocking soft sweetness.*) I was hoping it was you—doll! (*He listens. He sighs.*) But I don't know any other girls.

OLSON. (*To the boys.*) That boy is smooth!

TUB. (*With some reluctance.*) Beaumont is not bad—sometimes—

FUDGE. (*Who adores* BEAUMONT *twenty-four hours a day.*) Not bad? He's perfect.

BEAUMONT. (*Still into phone.*) You mustn't kid me—really you mustn't. You know what I'm afraid of, don't you? With you, I'm always afraid I'm the one who's gonna get hurt.

[41]

OLSON. He has more luck with that line than any of his other ones. I like the slap-happy one better but the dames like this.

BEAUMONT. (*Now looking at* WORMY *with mock severity. His tone is shocked to the girl on the phone.*) I cannot understand it. I never heard a thing like this about Weldy before. Oh, it must have been her fault. He is definitely not that type fellow. Try to think of somebody else. See you tonight—doll! (*He hangs up and walks over to* WORMY—*regards him curiously.*) Now where did you ever meet McWhinney?

WORMY. (*Blankly.*) McWhinney! McWhinney! Who's that?

WORMY. Johnson's cousin—Bernice McWhinney. She lives away over on the south side.

WORMY. Oh, her—I forgot all about her. I wouldn't even know her if she walked in that door.

BEAUMONT. (*Shaking his head at him.*) SHE remembers you. I gather you made quite an impression; the wrong impression, but deep, Fofo, deep. (*He lays his hand on* WORMY'S *shoulder. He speaks tenderly but as always there is a mocking note in his voice.*) Didn't we tell you, Weldy, you don't take a woman out, stare fixedly at her for ten minutes, and then make one of those lustful leaps?

CARNEY. (*He is doing push-ups on the floor. He now looks up at* WORMY.) Wormy, your trouble is lust.

TUB. (*Innocently.*) That's trouble?

WORMY. (*Wearily.*) Listen, it wasn't that way at all. Nothing like that at all. What are you guys trying to do—make me out a plain heel, some kind of a coarse character? (*He faces them and his chin is thrust out belligerently. They all grin at each other.*) Look, I took her to a dance. On the way home, I parked. We're sitting there in the front seat. I look at her and something comes over me. But what comes over me is not what you

[42]

think, because I ask myself—"Wormy, what's come over you? Are you on the make?" Then I answer myself—"No, sir. The thing to do is not to look at her just like she was a sharp-looking babe." So I say—"This is another lost soul, lonely and lost, just like me." So I grab for her, so she won't feel so lost. But she don't know she's lost and she shoves me away. Then I think—"Aw, nuts, if they don't even know when they're lost." I shove her back and we get into an argument.

CARNEY. (*After a moment's silence.*) Wormy, your name among the women in this town and surrounding suburbs is about as gladsome as Jack the Ripper's.

BEAUMONT. (*Softly.*) Gladsome—I like that word.

CARNEY. My old man's always saying it, especially when he's had a couple of snorts and wants to show off before company.

BEAUMONT. It takes me back to English 47 in which I am also flunking. (*At this point,* KINSWOOD *enters from the left. He is carrying a dachshund in his arms.* FUDGE *sees him first and rises menacingly.*)

FUDGE. Git outta heah!

KINSWOOD. Weldy, are you coming home? (*Now all of the boys see* KINSWOOD *and an expression of disdain comes over their faces—except* BEAUMONT's. *He regards* KINSWOOD *with amused detachment.*)

TUB. (*Rising and going toward him.*) Beat it, Kinswood. Wanta get hurt?

KINSWOOD. (*Not budging.*) Don't flatter yourselves I want to hang around you guys. I wouldn't lower myself.

WORMY. (*Jumping up, his face flushed with anger.*) Listen, Kinswood, none of your cracks to my friends—see!

KINSWOOD. (*Facing him but still not budging.*) You know how

[43]

your mother feels about these guys. (*To the boys.*) He's got homework to do. He's supposed to be home doing it right now.

FUDGE. (*Coming closer.*) I told you—git outta heah!

KINSWOOD. (*He does turn and start for the exit. Stops.*) I wouldn't even step inside this dive if I didn't feel sorry for Mrs. Weldy.

WORMY. Sorry! Sorry for her? Why? Nobody holds a clock on her.

KINSWOOD. You promised her you'd be gone only long enough to take your dog for a walk.

WORMY. (*Now completely outraged. He hurries over to* KINSWOOD *and takes the dog from him; holds him up and speaks to him.*) You old pot you—you stinking old—

BEAUMONT. (*With one leap crosses and takes the dog from him.*) Weldy, you slob, that's no way to talk to a swell dog like this. You can feel the little guy's heart beating. He's scared. (*He pets the dog tenderly. The other boys gather around to pet the dog and glare at* WORMY.)

WORMY. (*How he would like to like the dog! How he does like him! But to show it is defeat. He pats the dachshund's head and speaks slowly.*) Do you know what you're supposed to represent? You've been tricked too. (*The dog drops his head as though ashamed.*) You're supposed to be a substitute for a glamorous female woman in my life. I'm not taking it. No sir. (*Takes the dog from* BEAU *and gives him to* KINSWOOD.) Take him home, Kinswood.

FUDGE. I told you before, Kinswood. (*He reaches for his collar.* KINSWOOD *ducks and runs out quickly. The boys all laugh loudly.*)

WORMY. (*Running to the exit and calling after him.*) And if you pop where I am, I'll clean you, Kinswood. I swear, I'll mess you up.

TUB. Oh, how I despise that dumb moose.

CARNEY. Who doesn't?

WORMY. My old lady. That's how she planned my evening; homework with Kinswood, cold chicken, and chocolate milk. Oh, I have nothing against her personally. It's just that she interferes with me. If she wasn't related to me, I might even think she was a pretty good joe.

BEAUMONT. Up in Sneaky Falls, the mothers and the boys are not even members of the same family. It works perfect.

WORMY. (*Bitterly.*) She's always half a mile behind me. When I wanted a car, she bought me a tool chest. When I want a girl, she buys me a dog. Drove me out to the country yesterday. "Buford," she says, "pick one out." I'm dreaming of babes and she's pointing to dachshunds. Well, nuts, he was the last straw. I made up my mind I was sneaking out and getting a date tonight if it kills me. (*He walks back and forth, frowning, his hands in his pockets. The boys watch him and listen placidly. Now he stops and pounds on the table with his fist.*) And top this for humiliation! My old lady has got a date tonight and I can't get one.

BEAUMONT. (*Seriously.*) Now, listen Wormy, don't you believe it. I've watched these old characters. They don't have dates. They have seating arrangements. They get into the same car, ride to the same place, and get out. And they do it alphabetically, too. Your old lady probably filled out an application blank that came in the mail. But she hasn't got a date, Wormy, don't let her fool you. (*There is a ring at the telephone.* OLSON *runs to answer it.*)

OLSON. Climax Laundry. Keep it clean. (*As he listens his eyes grow wide with amazement. He hangs up the receiver and speaks in an awesome tone.*) The Reindeer has got a date tonight! (*They all receive this news with a loud groan.*)

WORMY. (*After a moment.*) Oh well, let me think. What about you, Olson, do you know anybody?

OLSON. Any girls, you mean? Well, there's my sister but she's an awful drip. I'd hate to wish it on a friend of mine.

TUB. (*The expert speaks.*) I've seen her. She's pretty cute.

WORMY. Call her, Dink, will you call her? Ask her if she's got a date and if she has, ask her if she'll break it?

OLSON. Got a date? She never HAS had a date.

TUB. How old is she?

OLSON. I don't know. Fourteen, I think.

WORMY. (*Sagging again.*) Let it go. Thanks just the same, Dink. There must be somebody, somewhere. Look, Carney—

TUB. The trouble is you've already met so many of them. You are a kind of a blight.

WORMY. (*He sits down in the chair center stage.*) Yeah! I wonder if this stuff is hereditary. I wonder how my old man got by. If I knew for sure he'd been a slob with women I wouldn't worry so much. But I can't ask him. He's married again and lives out in Pasadena.

CARNEY. He wouldn't tell you if you did ask him. They never tell you anything really important like that.

OLSON. Which is why you can never tell them anything really important.

CARNEY. Of course, they try to sneak up on you and get information. The other night after that beer bust at Rivertown, both of them pushed me into a corner and coaxed me to confide. (*He raises a clenched fist on the word "coax."*)

WORMY. (*He has not been listening to his friends. His mind has been far, far off searching for something. Now he seems to have found it. He jumps up.*) I've got it. Now I know. I know what I'll do.

CARNEY. He's got that reckless look on his face. Now, Wormy, you're not gonna try to get a date with Jean Cantrick!

WORMY. Cantrick! Are you crazy? (*He is genuinely shocked.*)

OLSON. Cantrick! She's dated months in advance.

WORMY. Listen, desperate as I am, that is the one babe and the only one I wouldn't take a date with, for all the salt in the ocean. A lot of 'em may turn me down but HER I turn down. So forget it.

BEAUMONT. (*Smiling.*) The boy is so violent. He may be fond.

WORMY. Fond? Fond of Cantrick? She is a coral snake. I've been raised with her. There isn't a thing about her I don't know and it's all bad.

CARNEY. She's Langley's girl anyway.

WORMY. She can be anybody's. She'll never be mine. (*His eyes for one brief second stare off into space. Then he moves impatiently and begins to walk across the stage in great excitement.*) Listen! I've turned a corner. I am about to stop brooding and start living. (*He grabs for his coat.*) Why it's as clear as day. (*He takes his necktie from the coat pocket and ties it around his neck as he speaks.*) What I've got to do is forget these jerks and move up into more sophisticated circles. I'm going to get myself a date tonight with a really hep older woman.

BEAUMONT. (*Very interested.*) Yeah? Who? (*All the boys move forward to hear the answer to this question.*)

WORMY. (*Getting into his coat.*) I don't know, but I will. I've got fifty bucks (*He slaps his hip pocket*), right here next to my draft card. Fifty bucks my old man sent me for Christmas. Nuts with these jerks in blue jeans and sloppy socks. What I'm after is the slinky stuff with the come-on look and the warm, warm glance.

OLSON. Who ain't? Know anybody?

WORMY. (*He takes a pocket comb out of his coat pocket and pulls it through his hair.*) Someone—someone who doesn't know my name is mud, so I'll change my name. I'm going out now and stand on a street corner. She'll come along. She's got to come along.

TUB. Weldy, you're crazy! You'll get thrown in jail.

WORMY. Where the hell do you think I am now?

OLSON. Listen, Wormy—!

WORMY. Oh no, don't try to talk me out of it. I'm tired of being a joke. (*He walks back to the boys who stand in a group watching him, in amazement.*) I'm tired of schoolgirls slapping my face. I want to live, like you guys. (*He wheels around sharply and starts out.*)

BEAUMONT. (*Following him.*) Wait a minute, Wormy.

WORMY. (*At the exit.*) I'm waiting no more; because somewhere in this town there's a woman who'll relax in my arms. When I enfold her, she'll stay folded—A woman—well, even if she feels like pushing me away—she'll have character enough not to do it—(*He looks out toward the street.*) So, Bernardine— be there—be there—! So long, fellows, thanks for the try— (*He runs out quickly. The boys watch him open-mouthed with amazement. The lights dim.*)

BLACKOUT

TIME: *A half hour later.*

SCENE: *A section of the lobby of the Barclay Hotel, the best hotel in town. There is a lush, plush expanse of red carpet, marble columns, gold wall brackets, and potted palms. Center stage there is a circular red plush ottoman built around the center column. The hotel orchestra in the dining room near by plays Strauss music. Every now and then there is the sound of elevator doors closing off right, and bellboys paging. There are entrances backstage left and right and downstage left and right, leading to different parts of the lobby.*

WORMY is seated on the ottoman languidly. He takes a piece of gum out of his pocket and is about to tear off the wrapper when a young woman enters the lobby and walks across. She is handsome and wears a close-fitting black satin dress.

He stuffs the gum back into his pocket and follows her off, giving her the heels-to-head close scrutiny he gives all females.

They both disappear.

From the other side of the stage enters CARNEY. He runs around the ottoman, peers left and right, and finally stops. Then he runs to the center and calls loudly:

"Hey, guys. In here. I found him. He's here."

OLSON, TUB, *and* FUDGE *enter on the run, followed by* BEAU-MONT. *Two men in business suits, wearing black homburgs and carrying brief cases, cross and stare curiously at this gang of boys without neckties, wearing blue jeans and suede jackets. The boys are oblivious of the impression they're making and they form a cluster at one side of the stage, staring off stage.*

A BELLBOY *crosses wearing a red suit with gold braid.*

BELLBOY. Calling Mr. Kratke. Calling Mr. Kratke. (*He sees the gang of boys, turns and goes back toward the manager's office.*)

TUB. (*To* BEAU.) See him. There he is down by the porter's desk. He just got the brush from the chick in the black dress and now he's trying the tomato in pink.

BEAUMONT. Standing behind her—hovering—like Dracula! (*They watch silently a moment, then groan and part.* BEAU *shakes his head and goes to sit on the ottoman.*

TUB. Did you see that stupe? He stiffens his jaw like a prize fighter and goes up to that tomato like this. (TUB *thrusts his jaw forward like Mussolini and pokes* BEAU'S *arm with a stiff forefinger.*)

BEAUMONT. (*Nodding.*) Just like a house dick.

CARNEY. Oh—oh—look at her squelch him! (*At this point the hotel* MANAGER *enters. He is a rotund little fellow wearing a morning coat and black cutaway. He ambles past the boys and gives them a suspicious eye. As he crosses the stage he keeps glancing back at them. He goes out.*)

CARNEY. (*Reporting to the others about* WORMY.) He's trying the other side of the lobby now!

FUDGE. Let's see.

CARNEY. Cut it—who you shovin'.

FUDGE. Careful, son. (*He picks* CARNEY *up and swings him downstage. They wrestle and fall to the floor in a roughhouse.*)

[52]

OLSON. (*Jumping up.*) Hey, you guys, cut it. Cut it. That manager just gave us a dirty look. Oh—oh—here he comes. Let's blow. (*They all make a move to leave quickly but* BEAU *rises slowly.*)

BEAUMONT. Don't—move. (*They freeze in their positions as the* MANAGER *again enters the lobby. This time he approaches them. He is very affable. He has that "let's handle this quietly" type of unctious smile.*)

MANAGER. Good afternoon, boys.

BEAUMONT. (*Very respectfully.*) Good afternoon, sir.

MANAGER. (*Looking carefully at their clothes.*) Well, well—are you boys waiting for someone?

BEAUMONT. Yes, sir. My grandfather, sir. I believe he's reserved a suite on the seventh floor.

MANAGER. R. K. Spofford? Oklahoma City? Five o'clock train?

BEAUMONT. (*Feigning admiration for his omniscience.*) Why, yes, sir!

MANAGER. He's on eight. Eight sixty-five. Just make yourselves at home, boys. (*He pats* BEAU'S *shoulder and walks off beaming.*)

CARNEY. (*To* OLSON *in low tone.*) He flunks in everything at school but get him in a tough spot and Beaumont is a king.

BEAUMONT. Now up in Sneaky Falls they pay the boys to come in and throw fire crackers in the revolving doors of the good hotels.

OLSON. I've always wanted to earn my keep throwing paper bags full of cold water across the transoms of the rest rooms.

BEAUMONT (*Tenderly patting his head.*) Up in Sneaky Falls we have a place for an ambitious boy like you. (WORMY *enters from stage right. He looks up and sees the boys and is at first*

[53]

delighted. Then a worried expression crosses his face as he looks again. CARNEY *is now posing, hand on hip, like a statue beside one of the potted palms.* FUDGE *and* OLSON *are doing a high wide waltz to the music.* TUB *is stretched out prone on the floor, his feet on the ottoman, his arms under his head.* BEAU *is wielding an imaginary baton. Two old women crossing the lobby are craning their necks and staring at this display.*)

WORMY. Hey, what are you guys doing here? How did you know I was here?

CARNEY. We saw you come in.

BEAUMONT. How is business, Fofo—little slow?

WORMY. (*Sighs.*) No luck yet. Say, have you guys seen anything interesting?

BEAUMONT. Yes.

WORMY. (*Eagerly.*) Yeah? Yeah?

BEAUMONT. The manager. We just saw HIM.

WORMY. (*Let down.*) Oh, well, this takes time. Look, you guys, don't stay close to me. Keep back. You don't fit with the line I'm using. I am now an orphan from Idaho about to be inducted into the navy and shipped to South America for seven years.

TUB. Saaay. That's a pretty smooth line. Figure that one out yourself?

BEAUMONT. He got it from a movie we saw last week. Only in the movie it was not a line. It was legitimate. This fellow met this mouse and they spent a really significant evening. Both doomed, of course.

CARNEY. (*Yawning.*) Of course. (WORMY *now sees a woman approaching and he shoves the boys, telling them to blow. In retaliation they pick him up and pitch him through the air to* FUDGE *who catches him. But they run out of the lobby laugh-*

ing. All except BEAU, *who listens a moment to the music and says in perfect seriousness to* WORMY—)

BEAUMONT. Get that phrase in there! Strauss had something. Not much—but something. (*He saunters out.*) (*The woman now enters. She wears a yellow cocktail dress and black lace hat.* WORMY *stalks her and is about to reach out and touch her when she sees someone she knows across the lobby—calls out "darling—here I am" and runs away.* WORMY's *shoulders slump and he goes over to the ottoman and sinks down on it. He leans back wearily and closes his eyes.*

Now enters a pretty young girl of about seventeen wearing a blue dirndl skirt and white peasant blouse. She is as fresh and wholesome as a spring morning. This is JEAN CANTRICK. *She sees* WORMY *and stops in front of him.*)

JEAN. Buford Weldy!

WORMY. (*This voice! Had he been dreaming of it as his eyes were closed? At any rate he jumps as though a fire cracker had exploded at his feet. He sees her and his eyes narrow. He goes "humph" and turns his head away, folding his arms across his chest.*)

JEAN. (*Walking over to him.*) What are you doing, sitting in this hotel lobby?

WORMY. (*Sullenly.*) Trying to pick up a fast woman—what do you think?

JEAN. (*Gasping.*) Well! I always knew you were loathsome and repulsive, but I didn't know you were absolutely rotten. (*But with one movement she sits down beside him and stares at him. He doesn't look at her. As far as he is concerned the ottoman is empty. She waits—and then finally speaks.*) Besides I don't believe you.

JEAN

[55]

(*He says nothing, stares ahead of him. She looks at him closely and moves a little uneasily. Buford is so strange. This isn't like him.*) I don't believe there are any women like that in here. (*He puts his hand to his mouth to stifle an imaginary yawn, then rises from the ottoman and walks to the entrance and looks out across the lobby with a man-of-the-world air. She follows and stands beside him—piqued.*) What are you staring at? Is that—one of those women—the one down at the desk there?

WORMY. (*In a low tone as though to himself.*) Rather nice that— um—hum—quite nice. (*He starts to go out after the woman and then stops.*) Nuts, she got in the elevator. Too bad. Oh well. There'll be others.

JEAN. (*She has been staring at him in amazement.*) I saw her. I thought she looked terrible. (WORMY *goes back and sits on the ottoman. She follows him. She scrutinizes him carefully. He continues to ignore her—yawns again.*) I could walk like she did. There's nothing special about that. Anybody could do that. Think I can't?

WORMY. (*He flicks an imaginary speck off his lapel and takes out a cigarette—gives a sarcastic laugh.*) Cantrick, I wouldn't make myself ridiculous in public if I were you.

JEAN. (*Stung.*) All right, just for that I'll just show you.

WORMY. Oh, go home and cut out your paper dolls.

JEAN. I'll show you. Now you watch. (*She fixes her body into what she considers a sexy pose; hips swung out, arm extended stiffly holding handbag, an artificial smile on her face. She walks out mincingly.*

WORMY *jumps up quickly and moves to look after her, but afraid that she may turn and see him watching her, he gets back onto the ottoman just as she returns with the same smile and movement. But now she is followed by a middle-aged man.*

He has a wolfish grin. He is a typical hotel lobby lounger in a striped suit, loud shirt and tie. JEAN *does not realize he is behind her. She sits on the ottoman beside* WORMY *and takes a compact out of her purse. She is very pleased with herself.*) Well—I did it.

WOLF. (*Leering and leaning over to her. His voice is soft.*) Hi, baby!

JEAN. (*She sees him and is delighted. She gives* WORMY *a "see there" look.*) Hello! Did you see me walk up to the porter's desk just now?

WOLF. (*Touching her arm.*) That I did, baby, that I did. (WORMY *is now watching this covertly out of the corner of one eye. Somehow he doesn't like it.*)

JEAN. (*Getting uneasy.*) Take your hand off my arm. Let go.

WOLF. (*Looks warily around the lobby but does not release her.*) Quiet, sweet, I live in this town. (*Rises and tries to pull her to her feet at the same time.*) Let's go!

JEAN. (*Now frightened.*) Stop it. You stop it. Stop pulling me.

WOLF. (*Menacingly.*) Skip the act, kid.

JEAN. (*Now tearful.*) Let go—you're hurting me.

WORMY. (*Jumping up suddenly, seizing hold of the* WOLF's *arm.*) Leave her alone!

WOLF. (*Still has hold of* JEAN.) Beat it, kid—

WORMY. Says who?

WOLF. Me. (*He gives* WORMY *a fierce shove.* WORMY *hauls off and hits him hard in the jaw. The* WOLF *drops* JEAN's *arm. She runs out as he steps back to swing on* WORMY. *But from the left in a great rush—come* THE BOYS!

FUDGE *is in the lead and there is the joyful gleam of battle*

[57]

on his face. He grabs the WOLF *from behind and pinions both of his arms. The* WOLF *struggles in vain.* FUDGE *is not the gang ugh-me-fix for nothing, but since both his arms are busy* OLSON *obligingly leans over and thumps his chest for him—)*

OLSON. Ugh—you—fix!

BEAUMONT. (*Walks around and faces the* WOLF, *shakes his head sadly as he flips out the man's tie and goes "tsk—tsck—")* Shame—Shame—Shame!

WOLF. (*Struggling to get free.*) What is this—a racket? Witnick —Eddie—help—help!

BEAUMONT. Toss him, boys. (*All of the boys including* WORMY *surround the* WOLF *and push him toward the door like a stalled car. His yells become louder.*)

WOLF. Help—help—(*The* MANAGER *runs on stage followed by the* BELLBOY.)

MANAGER. Get Brady—a fight!

WOLF. Help—help—Witnick—

MANAGER. Get Louis—call the police—call the police! (*He runs off stage after the boys, followed by three bellhops and two elevator operators and a porter.*)

ALL. Fight! Fight! Fight!

BLACKOUT

TIME: *Immediately following.*

SCENE: *The Weldy living room.*

RUTH WELDY *and* SELMA CANTRICK *are having tea with a beautiful blonde woman in her early thirties. She wears a soft gray suit and small gray hat with a veil, charmingly draped. This glamorous looking creature is* ENID LACEY. *Her manner is relaxed. Her smile, slow and sweet.*

RUTH. (*Who leans across the tea table to her.*) Enid! Do you mean to tell me a perfectly strange boy walked right up to you in a hotel lobby in this town in broad daylight—

SELMA. And propositioned her. Isn't that something!

ENID. (*Her laugh is low and throaty.*) Yes. (*The telephone rings.*)

RUTH. (*As she goes to answer it.*) Maybe that's Buford now. I can't imagine what's keeping him. Hello. No, he isn't here, but I'm expecting them any minute. I'll tell him to call you, Mrs. Kinswood. (*She walks back to the girls.*) Now don't blame that boy, Enid. In a case like that—blame the parents. You've got to make a companion of a boy.

SELMA. But this boy told Enid he had no parents. He told her he was an orphan from Idaho about to be shipped off—wasn't that it, Enid?

ENID. Yes.

RUTH. What was he like, Enid?

ENID. (*She smiles as she remembers.*) So fresh—so young—only 22—and so—adorable!

ENID

RUTH. (*Her mind now back on her own boy.*) I wonder if they stopped in at the grocery store and got caught in the crowd. I'll call the library. (*She goes back to the telephone.*) I'm so anxious for you to meet him, Enid. Buford was only a toddler when you left here. You wouldn't know him now.

ENID. But, dear, of course I would.

RUTH. I'll try the reference room. (*She dials.*) Would you please look around your shelves and see if Buford Weldy is there? I'll wait.

SELMA. (*To Enid.*) It's a shame this sailor boy couldn't get a date with a girl his own age.

ENID. Oh yes.

RUTH. (*Still waiting at the telephone.*) A girl his own age! Let me tell you something, Enid. These modern girls won't go out with boys. I've seen my Buford stand at this phone on a Friday night and call number after number. This is a neurotic generation of young girls. Don't look at me like that, Selma. I mean your own daughter, too. Hello. He's not there? Thank you. (*Hangs up.*)

SELMA. Enid, why don't you get a date and come to the club dance with us tonight?

ENID. I am going—with Coakey Ferris.

[60]

RUTH. (*Joining her friends.*) Somehow that poor boy haunts me. (*She sits.*) When anything comes up concerning a boy I always have a little test I make. I say: "Now what if it were Buford?" (*She leans back and closes her eyes—as though going into a trance.*) Now, let me see. What if this were Buford? What if I were dead and Buford were 22, wandering around alone in a strange town about to be shipped off for seven years. (*Opens her eyes.*) I hope I can be completely honest about this. But I have to keep remembering I'm dead. (*Closes her eyes again and settles back against the sofa.*) And what if I were looking down upon him. (*Lifts up forefinger.*) I'm getting it. I know. I've got it. (*She speaks very slowly.*) I would hope that his guardian angel would lead him to some kind, sympathetic, lovely woman—so that means she'd have to be an older woman. And if he insisted on THAT experience I would want it to be for him something beautiful—something to ennoble him—not coarsen him. So that long afterward, even when he was happily married with a family—the memory of HER would flicker on down through the years like the flame of a candle in a dark cathedral. (*She sits silently a moment—her hands folded in her lap. While RUTH has been speaking, a curious rapt expression has settled on ENID's face. She leans forward thoughtfully. RUTH opens her eyes.*) I suppose you think I'm a silly romantic fool but that's how I'd feel.

SELMA. I would certainly call you romantic. There are no such women.

RUTH. Now don't you ever tell Laura Kinswood I said a thing like that. She'd be horrified. (*Speaking of Laura Kinswood, here is her boy, VERNON, standing now in the hallway with an expression of distress on his face.*)

KINSWOOD. (*Timidly in a loud whisper.*) Mrs. Weldy!

RUTH. (*She rises smiling.*) Oh, Vernon, there you are! Come in. Enid, this is Vernon Kinswood, Buford's chum. Mrs. Lacey.

ENID. Good afternoon.

RUTH. Tell Buford to come in here. I want him to meet Enid.

KINSWOOD. He didn't come home with me, Mrs. Weldy. But I brought the dog back.

RUTH. Where did he go, Vernon—to the library?

KINSWOOD. Well—uh—

RUTH. He did have a lot of things to look up this week end. I knew they didn't look carefully.

KINSWOOD. Mrs. Weldy—

RUTH. Yes, Vernon—

KINSWOOD. There's something I better speak to you about maybe—

RUTH. What is it, Vernon?

KINSWOOD. Maybe I'd better speak to you about it in the hall—

RUTH. Certainly, Vernon, I'll be right out—

KINSWOOD. (*Curious about* ENID.) Glad I met you. What was that name again? I always like to get the names because it cheers my mother up when I tell her who I've seen.

RUTH. Lacey. Enid Cranshawe Lacey. She used to live here and now she's come home to stay.

ENID. By way of Reno.

KINSWOOD. She always asks me what they're wearing too. What is that stuff?

SELMA. Tell her I had on a beige crepe and a felt hat, both last year's. What's yours, Enid?

ENID. Gray Adrian.

KINSWOOD. Thanks a lot—(*He goes into the hall, saying these materials to himself so as not to forget them.*)

RUTH. (*Following him.*) Excuse me—one moment.

SELMA. (*Rising.*) I've got to run. Can I drop you anywhere, Enid?

ENID. Thanks, dear, but I have my own car now. Got it last week.

SELMA. Did you finally decide on that powder-blue Cad convertible?

ENID. Yes.

SELMA. (*She goes to the door.*) By the way—why don't you and Coakey meet us at our place for a cocktail tonight—before the dance?

ENID. (*She is thoughtful.*) I may not go to the club tonight with Coakey after all. I have so much to do.

BLACKOUT

ACT ONE

SCENE 7

TIME: *Immediately following.*

SCENE: *The lobby of the Barclay Hotel.*

The boys stand in a group before the ottoman. They are being questioned by two policemen, one of whom holds a pad and pencil in his hand.

The MANAGER *looks sternly on the proceedings, his hands clasped behind his back. The* BELLBOY *stands beside him, frowning.*

The boys have their eyes on BEAUMONT. *He stands slightly forward from the group, facing the officer.*

BEAUMONT. (*His most respectful tone.*) You see, officer, we were sitting here, waiting, and we saw this character. He was over there—cutting little pieces out of the upholstery with a jack-knife about so big.

MANAGER. What?

BELLBOY. Why that crazy galoot!

MANAGER. (*Fuming.*) Psychopath—degenerate! Lock him up. Where is he?

COP. He got away from us.

BEAUMONT. (*Tolerantly.*) Oh, there is always that element.

MANAGER. They can stay out of here.

BEAUMONT. So we tossed him out.

MANAGER. Officer, I didn't understand the circumstances. Much obliged to you boys. Very much obliged.

BEAUMONT. Oh, that's perfectly all right. It's only part of our regular work.

COP. What's that?

BEAUMONT. (*Easily.*) You see, officer, we belong to a boys' club, The American Youth Watch Movement. We discourage the destruction of property in public places. Maybe you've heard of our work.

COP. (*Doubtfully.*) Seems to me maybe I did read something about it. That's fine work they're doing down there.

BEAUMONT. (*Turns to* TUB.) Give the officer one of our cards, Mr. Bidnut.

TUB. (*Slapping his pockets.*) Darn. I passed them all out at the depot this morning.

COP. (*To* MANAGER, *indicating slip he has been making out.*) You want me to tear this up now?

MANAGER. Of course, by all means. I misunderstood the circumstances. Boys, if you'll just step into my office and sign your names to a report for the insurance company I'll be very much obliged.

BEAUMONT. Glad to, sir—glad to—come on, fellows. (*The officers leave and the boys, all except* WORMY, *follow the* MANAGER *off stage into his office.*)

WORMY. (*He runs around calling.*) Jean—Oh Jean—!

JEAN. (*She slinks out from behind a marble column. She has been crying.*) Buford! Buford, I was scared.

[66]

WORMY. You better go on home.

JEAN. I'm afraid to go outside—that awful man!

WORMY. He's gone—we took care of him.

JEAN. Oh, what will my folks say?

WORMY. Who'll tell them?

JEAN. Oh, promise you'll never mention it.

WORMY. Oh yes, I'm liable to mention it. Oh sure, I'll get up in Chapel Monday and say: "Special announcement. Jean Cantrick was over at the Barclay Saturday afternoon—trying to pick up an old pot."

JEAN. (*Horrified.*) Buford—you wouldn't!

WORMY. Of course not. I'm not a pop-off like some people I know. I won't even tell Pete Langley.

JEAN. Now what do you mean by that, Buford Weldy?

WORMY. I think you know.

JEAN. So—he told you.

WORMY. He and I are about to tangle over it.

JEAN. I—well—maybe I did mention it, but I certainly didn't mean to make any trouble for you.

WORMY. Don't worry about me. Worry about your boy friend— I'll smear him.

JEAN. I guess you despise me, don't you?

WORMY. Oh, why talk about it? It's all ancient history now.

JEAN. There really is quite a nice side to you, Buford, when you want to be nice.

WORMY. When Pete Langley called me and informed me he was

waiting to pop me, he didn't happen to mention anything like that in the blast you gave him about me.

JEAN. Well—no matter what I did—you were worse.

WORMY. A creep like Langley! I should think you could do better than that. If it were a real fellow like Beau or Tub or Carney— And I've known you all my life! But to sell me out to a creep you've only known about six months—that was low!

JEAN. (*Uncertainly.*) You brought it on yourself, Buford. You made some pretty darned fresh passes the last time I was out with you.

WORMY. (*Now turning and looking her directly in the eye.*) I'm making no more passes at you—ever—Cantrick. You may have to worry about a lot of things but you'll never have to worry about that. To me—from now on—you are just Langley's goofy girl friend—and kid, he is certainly welcome to you. (*He turns away.*)

JEAN. (*His tone has been so final.*) Well! Well, I'm glad you reminded me. I've got a date with him in about an hour. (*She flounces off—looking back at* WORMY *but he has not turned— and so she has not seen the tears of angry hurt in his eyes. He kicks at the ottoman and sits down again, resting his chin on his hands, his arms propped on his knees. The boys now walk in, grinning. Each has a long, big black cigar in his mouth, courtesy of the management.* OLSON *has even lit his. He coughs.*)

BEAUMONT. (*Expansively in his deep, businessman's voice.*) The manager and his whole staff—fine men—all of them—fine, fine men!

CARNEY. (*To* WORMY.) Hey, what happened with you and that guy anyway?

WORMY. (*He has been thinking about* JEAN.) What? Oh. He was making a pass at a little squirt kid and so I popped him. He was pulling at her and mauling her.

[68]

BEAUMONT. Must have shocked you, Weldy, to see a man lay rough hands on a woman.

WORMY. An old pot like that! She wasn't doing a thing to him. She wasn't shoving him or hitting him or anything.

BEAUMONT. (*Shaking his head regretfully.*) She was yellow, huh? Afraid to fight! Well, some of them are.

CARNEY. (*With a sudden startled movement.*) Weldy! Here comes your old lady!

WORMY. (*Frantically.*) Oh, my God!

BEAUMONT. (*Instantly taking command.*) Close him in. (*To* WORMY.) Get down—we'll make a wall; squat. Fudge, get by me. Tub, stand here; Carney, here. Olson, close in. (WORMY *is now obscured from sight by the boys who stand stiffly in a semi-circle around him.*) Wormy, you there?

WORMY. (*Pushing his head out between their legs like an animal in a cage.*) Where the hell would I go?

BEAUMONT. Shh—back down—keep quiet.

WORMY. (*Again pushing his head out.*) I am quiet.

BEAUMONT. I can hear you breathing—stop it. Oh—oh—here she comes. (*Enter* RUTH WELDY, *followed by* KINSWOOD. *She is wearing a suit, and a small felt hat which she has apparently adjusted in great haste because it sits too far on one side of her head; and she is carrying a fox fur. Her manner, in contrast, is queenly. She sees the boys from across the stage, stops, and whispers to* KINSWOOD.)

RUTH. There THEY are.

KINSWOOD. I was sure of it when I saw Beaumont's old car outside.

RUTH. But where is Buford?

KINSWOOD. He WAS with them, Mrs. Weldy.

[69]

RUTH. Go look around the other side of the lobby. I'll speak to them but I won't let on a thing. (KINSWOOD *disappears quickly and* RUTH, *sauntering across the lobby, pretends great surprise when she looks up and sees them.*)

RUTH. Why—hello there, boys. (*The boys all get on their faces that weak, foolish look which they reserve for the parents of their friends and the friends of their parents. They look strained, uncomfortable; suddenly become awkward and inarticulate. They look at* RUTH, *murmur:* "Hello—well—" *and glance uncomfortably at each other.* RUTH *walks up and down before them like an officer inspecting a line of troops.*) How is your father, Arthur?

BEAUMONT. Oh—fine—just fine—thanks.

RUTH. (*To* TUB.) Marvin, I hear your sister's getting married this summer.

TUB. That's what she claims.

RUTH. (*To* CARNEY.) Leonard, I saw your mother in the beauty parlor the other day.

CARNEY. Well—well!

RUTH. We had a fine old gab fest about our boys.

CARNEY. That so? Well! Well!

RUTH. (*To* OLSON.) Morgan, I haven't seen you for a long time.

OLSON. That so—well!

RUTH. (*She comes to* FUDGE.) I thought I knew all of you boys but I don't believe I know this boy.

BEAUMONT. Mrs. Weldy, George Friedelhauser, George Friedelhauser, Mrs. Weldy.

RUTH. Happy to meet you. I am Buford Weldy's mother.

FUDGE. Okay—okay. Sure.

RUTH. It's a lovely afternoon, boys, isn't it?

BOYS. (*In murmuring chorus.*) Sure is—my yes—sure, sure.

RUTH. But it looked for a while as though it might rain.

BEAUMONT. It certainly looked that way.

CARNEY. Sure looked like rain awhile ago.

OLSON. I said to myself—that's rain.

FUDGE. Aw, I knew it wouldn't rain. (*Now to their dismay* RUTH *goes over and sits on the ottoman. She leans back against the plush and languidly surveys the lobby.*)

RUTH. I love to walk through this lobby. I love this hotel. I used to come here to dances when I was a girl.

BOYS. Well—that so? Well!

RUTH. How are your folks, Morgan?

OLSON. Oh—fine, thanks. How's yours—I mean—how is Buford?

RUTH. (*This convinces her* BUFORD *is not with them. She rises.*) What? Oh, Buford is fine, thank you. He had a little trouble getting adjusted this semester, but he's gradually learning to assume his responsibilities and he's beginning to realize that people get old soon enough and none of us can rush our development and we should be content to be boys as long as we can. (*They stand silently, saying nothing now.* RUTH *sees* KINSWOOD *entering the lobby from across the stage. She says good-by to the boys and hurries over to him.*) Did you find him? (KINSWOOD *shakes his head.* WORMY, *behind the stockade, thinking she has gone—sticks his head out again.*)

WORMY. She gone?

BEAUMONT. (*Warningly, his eyes on* KINSWOOD *and* RUTH, *who are still standing at the other side of the stage.*) The cruel hawk lurks near by while the dumb little bird chirps in the branches.

WORMY. I asked you—what gives? (*He pushes his head out again.*)

BEAUMONT. (*With more ice in his tone.*) The dumb little bird had better stop chirping. If the cruel hawk doesn't get him—the trees will.

RUTH. (*Looking over and smiling.*) Did you speak to me, Arthur?

BEAUMONT. No, I didn't, Mrs. Weldy! (*Now they are faced with another crisis, for the hotel* MANAGER *on one of his frequent inspections of the lobby comes in and walks slowly by the boys, puzzled by the odd formation in which they are standing. He saunters over to look behind the wall they have made of themselves. To prevent his seeing anyone there, the boys begin to inch gradually clockwise to coincide with the movement of the* MANAGER. *But now they are in a dilemma. If they continue to do this—they will hide him from the hotel* MANAGER *but expose him to his mother.*

They glance nervously at BEAU *for directions. His face is pale. The explosion may come any minute now. What to do?*

Suddenly they are saved! RUTH *turns her back and goes away with* KINSWOOD, *saying to him as she departs:*

"Really there is something awfully odd about the way they're standing there."

The MANAGER, *who has seen* WORMY *hiding, does not understand any of it and so decides not to worry about it. He saunters off stage too.*

The boys break ranks, stretching and groaning from the strain.)

WORMY. Olson, you verminous louse; you crawling, putrid creature. (*Mimics.*) How is Buford?

BEAUMONT. (*Stroking* WORMY'S *head.*) He wanted to know and he couldn't ask you. Look, Wormy, I've been thinking. Why not give up?

WORMY. No sir. It's not only that I said I would and I will, but it's something else too. I'm waiting for someone special. The very first one I saw this afternoon. I followed her in here. (*His eyes glow.*) She was wearing a kind of gray veil—misty, dreamy—gorgeous. I can't forget her.

BEAUMONT. There are other things in a man's life besides women, Fofo—there's girls.

WORMY. (*He hasn't heard.*) She gave me the brush but I don't care. Maybe she'll come back—I'm gonna take a look on the other side of the lobby. See you! (*Hands in pockets, he goes out.*)

BEAUMONT. (*He pulls* TUB *downstage away from the others and whispers to him.*) Let's break it up. I think Olson's bum leg is giving him some trouble.

TUB. He didn't say anything about it.

BEAUMONT. And don't you. It hurts his pride. (*He saunters over to the others, affecting his man-of-the-world air.*) I've got to blow. I don't pay any room and board out there but they get upset if I miss one meal—weird people! (*The boys make motions of departure and are about to exit when across the stage comes the* BELLBOY *again calling a page. He is carrying a jack and plug telephone in his arm.*)

BELLBOY. Call for Mr. Kratke. Call for Mr. Kratke.

BEAUMONT. (*One last laugh.*) Right here, boy. (*He pushes* FUDGE *forward.*)

BELLBOY. (*He looks at* FUDGE *suspiciously.*) You—Mr. Kratke?

FUDGE. (*Grinning at him.*) Always have been.

BELLBOY. Mr. Ogden Kratke?

BEAUMONT. Give Oggie his call, boy. (*Still dubious but also helpless the* BELLBOY *plugs the telephone into the wall and carries it to* FUDGE. *He is not hopeful but he waits for a tip anyway.*)

BEAUMONT. (*Pats his shoulder.*) And a very Merry Christmas! (*The* BELLBOY *goes off stage cursing under his breath.*)

FUDGE. (*Grins as he lifts the receiver. The boys are gathered closely around him like a Glee Club about to burst into song.*) Hello. (*To boys.*) She says: "Ogden, this is Mother!"

BEAUMONT. (*Sonorously.*) Glad to hear it. This is Father.

FUDGE. This is Father. (*To boys—his hand over the instrument.*) "Dad, how was the golf game?"

BEAUMONT. It was tender. It was real.

FUDGE. (*In phone.*) It was tender. It was real. (*To boys.*) "Dad, have you been drinking?"

BEAUMONT. Oh—not much. Have you? Be firm now.

FUDGE. Oh, not much. What about you—slob? (*Drops instrument and jumps back as though burned.*) Boy—do dames talk like that?

BEAUMONT. Dear old Ogden Kratke! Oh well, has he always played the game fair?

BOYS. NEVAH!!

BEAUMONT. You done fine, Fudge.

BOYS. You were great. (FUDGE *beams happily.*) (*At this point now entering the lobby, wearing a long white satin gown and a short white ermine jacket, her golden hair falling softly around her neck—is* ENID!

The effect of her upon the boys comes with the suddenness of an earthquake. They gape, they gasp, they stagger against each other, and from each throat emerges a primitive rumble,

[74]

rising and swelling and exploding into a roar. She seems not to hear or see. Her head is high and she walks swiftly across and then she's gone!)

BEAUMONT. (*Gasping.*) Bernardine! (*He runs off stage after her.*)

BOYS. (*Echoing him.*) Bernardine! (*In a mad rush and scramble, they run off stage following him.*) (ENID *has apparently made a short survey of the other side of the lobby and now she comes back from behind the columns backstage, walking behind the ottoman. She stands a moment, not realizing* BEAUMONT *is following her, looks around, sits down on the ottoman, and serenely adjusts the folds of her gown.*

The boys, who have followed BEAUMONT, *hide themselves behind the column and peer around to watch as he approaches her.*)

BEAUMONT. (*He pretends great humility.*) Excuse me! (*Surprised she looks up at him and turns her head away.*) I know I shouldn't have followed you. I knew it was wrong. (*The boys are peeking from behind the column, leaning out far. With one hand he waves them back.*) But I couldn't help it. Honest I couldn't. I guess—I guess you'll do strange things when you're in a strange town. Ever been to Idaho? That's my home. (*A curious expression flickers across* ENID's *face. She lets her eyes, now cold with disdain, rest on* BEAUMONT's *face.*)

ENID. Your parents?

BEAUMONT. I—I—never saw them—and they—they never saw me.

ENID. No?

BEAUMONT. I'm not complaining, but it's a little grim to be going where I'm going, with no fond farewells. But what's that to the U.S. Navy. (*He sits down beside her.*) Couldn't we go some place and talk—some place where I could just look at you?

[75]

ENID. (*Rising.*) NO. (*The boys behind the column, surprised by the force of her "no," tumble in a heap on the floor.* BEAU, *chagrined, has retreated quickly out of the lobby and they follow him.* ENID *walks to the opposite side and signals to a bellboy. She gives him a tip.*) Please call Mr. Ferris at the Athletic Club and tell him Mrs. Lacey WILL meet him at the Country Club right away. (*She turns, walks across the lobby and is about to go out when* WORMY, *entering from the other side, sees her and calls out.*)

WORMY. (*In awed, worshipful tone.*) Hello, hello, hello!

ENID. (*She is stopped by the sound of this voice. She turns and sees him across the stage; looks at him with contemptuous amusement. And this is the boy she actually allowed herself to pity and romanticize, and for whom she broke a date with an old friend, a middle-aged banker who has adored her for years and now wants to marry her. Oh well! It was a lesson to her. All males are alike.*)

WORMY. (*Knowing nothing of these thoughts, walks to her beaming.*) Gorgeous, gorgeous, gorgeous. I didn't dream I'd ever see you again, but was I hoping—was I hoping!

ENID. (*Playing with him. She puts a thoughtful finger to her cheek and nods her head.*) Oh yes. I remember now. You're the boy without parents who is being shipped off to South America tomorrow—the boy who doesn't know a person in town?

WORMY. Maybe, but sugar, you and I are not going to spend the evening in conversation. Let's get that straight.

ENID. (*Shocked, incredulous.*) What! What did you say?

WORMY. (*Shaking his head and smiling down at her.*) And no looking at pressed flowers in books.

ENID. (*She smiles despite herself. This is the most impudent character she has ever met.*) Oh, you wouldn't like that?

[76]

WORMY. No listening to the radio, either.

ENID. (*At least he is different.*) So that's out, too.

WORMY. And so is yakkin' with the old folks. Not with you and me, gorgeous. Uh-uh—never—never.

ENID. (*Just how shall she flatten this one? He deserves something special in the way of a squelch—but what?*) Well—at least you're honest. I'll say that for you.

WORMY. (*He comes closer to her. His voice is low and intimate.*) And I'm no chicken, doll. You scared?

ENID. (*As she looks into his blue eyes, at his fresh, firm skin, she is about to burst into laughter. But she doesn't. There is something about this boy. She felt it at once when he approached her this afternoon. She is surprised at the words she hears faltering from her lips.*) Why I—I don't really quite know what I am.

WORMY. (*Seriously.*) I do. You're a dream and I've been waiting for you—all my life.

ENID. (*After a moment.*) That hasn't been so long—has it?

WORMY. Oh no—just forever—that's all. Shall we go—doll?

ENID. (*She has decided. She puts her hand on his arm and smiles up at him.*) Yes. Why not?

WORMY. (*His heart has stopped beating.*) Oh, Bernardine—at last. At last. (*He sighs with ecstasy and walking on a cloud he guides her across the lobby and they go out.*) (*At this, the boys, BEAU in the lead, stagger across the stage peering after them—amazed, aghast. WELDY! WELDY and Bernardine! BEAU pretends to fall. The other boys prop him up as he lifts a trembling forefinger and points off stage after the departing couple.*)

CURTAIN

Act II

ACT TWO

SCENE I

TIME: *About twenty minutes later.*

SCENE: ENID LACEY'S *apartment.*

The room is empty. There is a light from the street outside filtering through the curtains at the window.

This room is exquisite, like the inside of a jewel box. The crystal chandelier hanging from the ceiling glitters in the dim light and we see the outlines of a small sofa center stage, coffee table, end tables, and occasional chairs with slender carved legs. The carpeting is thick and all over. The draperies are voluminous, hanging to the floor.

There is the sound of a key turning in the lock. The door at backstage opens and ENID *enters. She turns on a light switch. The colors in this room are pink and ivory. She comes in and removes her white ermine coat, throwing it casually over the back of a chair.*

WORMY *enters slowly, looking everywhere curiously.* ENID *turns and walks toward the door.*

WORMY. Hey—I mean—wait. (*She stops.*) Where are you going?

ENID. (*In low tone.*) I thought I'd just lock the outside door.

[81]

WORMY. (*With what he assumes to be a man-of-the-world shrug.*) Oh—sure—sure—why naturally. (*She smiles at him and goes out.*) (*He straightens his tie, walks to the window, peers out, walks to the other side of the room, tries a door there, stops and draws a hand across his brow. He takes out a cigarette, lights it, drops the match on the floor, then guiltily picks it up and puts it in his coat pocket.* ENID *walks back in, goes behind a mirrored screen upstage.*) Well—ah—well—whose place is this?

ENID. (*She comes from behind the screen carrying a silver tray with a decanter of wine and two tall-stemmed glasses.*) Mine.

WORMY. That so—it's nice.

ENID. Thank you.

WORMY. (*He is smoking furiously.*) Live here—alone?

ENID. (*She takes the tray to the coffee table in front of the little sofa and sets it down.*) Yes.

WORMY. I thought there might be some people—some other people living back there or in there or up there. (*He indicates each direction with a tilt of his head.*)

ENID. (*She sits on the sofa.*) No one. Please relax.

WORMY. Oh, I'm relaxed all right. I'm plenty relaxed. (*He sits stiffly at the other end of the sofa.*)

ENID. (*Handing him a glass.*) Wine? (*He takes it. She lifts hers high, looks at him, and smiles.*) Bon voyage!

WORMY. Beg your pardon!

ENID. (*There is a twinkle in her eye.*) Your trip—good sailing.

WORMY. (*He must not forget the line he gave her.*) Oh—that— thank you—same to you. (*He downs the wine in one gulp. She takes a slight sip of hers and turns to set the glass down on the table. As she turns sideways to do this, away from him, he gives her that close, narrow-eyed scrutiny he gives all women, intense, absorbed, detailed. He is like a cat ready to spring, watchful, hair-trigger tension, but he must choose the right moment. He half rises—should he spring now? She turns and looks at him and he sits back down on the sofa.*)

ENID. Can I get you something—a cigarette? (*She offers him a silver box.*)

WORMY. (*As he reaches for one.*) Say—ah—

ENID. Yes.

WORMY. I was going to say, you seem a lot taller in here than you did down there and this afternoon too. You seemed like a little bit of a woman then, Bernardine.

ENID. Bernardine—you've called me that twice tonight. My name is Enid. Who is Bernardine? (*She lights his cigarette.*) Your girl?

WORMY. Oh no. Not that.

ENID. But WHO is Bernardine?

WORMY. Oh, that's a kind of a name the fellows in my crowd have for a kind of a daydream. This fellow named Beaumont— ever run into him?

ENID. No, I don't think so.

WORMY. He made it up. Bernardine Crud, he always says.

ENID. (*Laughing.*) Bernardine Crud! Oh, how ridiculous!

WORMY. (*Very seriously.*) He's quite a character, Beaumont. He's a smooth operator. So is Griner—Tub Griner—ever happen to run into him?

ENID. No, I don't think so.

WORMY. They're my best friends and they're plenty big wheels, those boys.

ENID. Big wheels?

WORMY. Make time with women, know how to hold their liquor, and something else too—a kind of know-how—savvy, sharp, hep.

ENID. Are you a big wheel too, Ralph?

WORMY. (*Why does she call him Ralph—oh yes—he told her his name was Ralph Bidnut. He must remember this.*) Well, a guy doesn't like to say a thing like that about himself. If he ever should, you can be sure he's not a big wheel—keep that in mind.

ENID. I will. Tell me. (*She moves closer to him.*) How did you happen to come up to me this afternoon? Oh, I know you're going away and you're a stranger here, but how did you happen to decide to speak to me, especially?

WORMY. (*Amazed at this question.*) Why did I walk up to you? Oh Bernardine! (*He moves closer to her.*) Don't you know what you do to a guy? Don't you realize? Is it possible you don't know? I think that would be pretty obvious. You send him.

ENID. Send him? Where?

WORMY. Now, don't con me, you know where. Away off there, out there in the clouds. You're like a song floating by. You're dreamy. You make him want to trail behind you, follow you wherever you're going, and never, never, never come back to where he is.

ENID. (*After a pause.*) Don't you have a girl, Ralph? A girl your own age? You must know some.

WORMY. (*Evasively.*) Oh sure. I know plenty all right—but—

ENID. Don't you take them out—go dancing? You must do a lot of that—

[84]

WORMY. (*His head is down now. He clenches and unclenches his fists.*) Oh sure—I take them out. One at a time. First one—and uh—well, the other. But you get tired of the same old faces. These girls I know, I've known them so long. You know how these things are!

ENID. (*Nodding.*) Of course. You're bored with them.

WORMY. (*With feeling.*) Oh boy—am I bored with them!

ENID. When I was your age I wasn't bored with anything.

WORMY. No. I don't suppose so. I guess you could interest just about anybody you wanted to—anybody in the world—any time.

ENID. I wasn't bored—because I was miserable. I was so boy crazy.

WORMY. You—boy crazy? You should have run into me then, sugar—what a collision!

ENID. (*Still reminiscing.*)—so awkward—so over-anxious—the boys all ran away from me—but I kept running after them. (*She turns now to flick the ash from her cigarette into an ash-tray on the end table by her side of the sofa.* WORMY *again half rises to make a lunge at her but again he sits down as she turns back. She smiles a sweet smile at him.*)

WORMY. I wish you wouldn't smile at me like that!

ENID. Why not? Do you want me to frown at you?

WORMY. It would sure make it a lot easier. I'm more used to it.

ENID. (*Moving closer to him.*) But I don't want to frown at you. I want to smile at you. You make me want to smile more than anybody I've met in a long, long time.

WORMY. A big joke, eh?

ENID. Not at all. It's not that kind of a smile. Ralph, with these girls who bore you so—isn't there one of them you like?

WORMY. (*He leans back against the sofa.*) Oh, well, I—

ENID. There must be.

WORMY. (*Dropping his head and studying the floor.*) Not any more. There used to be one I could never stop thinking about. Saw her this afternoon, too. But she turned out to be an awful jerk. I was surprised too. Thought there was more to her than that.

ENID. I gather she didn't bore you.

WORMY. Well, for a long time she didn't. Then she got so she did. It's all in the past now. I'm through with her. I wouldn't pick her up off a dust heap. You see—she would keep jumping to conclusions; the dumb little drip. She wouldn't sit still and all I ever wanted to say to her—was—well, I'd take her out, understand?

ENID. Yes.

WORMY. And, of course, on the way home, I'd park. And then I'd put my arm around her, like this. (*Puts his arm around ENID.*) There was something I wanted to say to her. But she'd go—(*Here he pushes ENID violently over to the other side of the sofa. His face is fierce with memory.*) And then I'd get so darned burned up with her, I'd go— (*Makes another lunge, grabs ENID with even more violence over to him.*) And she'd go— (*Flings her back again—like a rag doll.*)

ENID. (*Alarmed—cries out.*) Oooooooh!

WORMY. (*Nods with approval at this shriek.*) That's it. She'd let out a yak—just like that—same thing. (ENID, *now frightened of him is about to slide off the other end of the sofa to escape from a madman. She stops as he continues in the same tone, not looking at her at all. He is staring into space.*) We'd be sitting in the car on a dark street with the light from the street lamp falling on her face. It made her skin look like wintertime and her hair blacker than soot. (*His voice becomes tender.*)

[86]

Oh, baby, do you know how nice you are? You're not the little snoot-face you pretend to be. You're sweet and I know just how sweet. Nobody knows you like I do. I'll always know you and even when you act jerky you can't fool me. You put on an act because you're afraid somebody will suspect what a sweet little jerk you are. Why do you do that, baby? Why do you do it with me? (*There is a pause. He knocks one clenched fist into the open palm of his other hand. The look on* ENID's *face as she listens to him has changed from fear to softness and sympathy.* WORMY *now looks at her, brought back to the present. He is shamefaced.*) Nertz—I must have been talking to myself!

ENID. (*Slowly.*) Yes, you were talking to yourself. And in more ways than one, I think.

WORMY. (*Thoughtfully.*) There's an awful lot of hatred in this sex stuff, isn't there? (*She nods.*) Is it always that way?

ENID. (*Leaning back against the sofa.*) You go along believing it's always that way until one day you look up and you see somebody standing before you. Then suddenly, oh, very suddenly, you feel like you've never felt before. You feel refreshed. The weariness of years drops away from you and you want to tell him everything you've learned, teach him everything you know, forgetting yourself, even your own name. (*She looks pointedly at* WORMY *now.*)

WORMY. (*He doesn't understand that the "somebody" is himself.*) So, if after a while you get to the place where a thing like that happens to you—what's in it for you?

ENID. Everything—nothing—

WORMY. I don't know. I don't believe I could go for that. Sounds —well—kind of one-sided—kind of softheaded.

ENID. Perhaps it is. Yes, I'm sure it is. (*She laughs and rests her head against the back of the sofa, closing her eyes.* WORMY *now changes his position on the sofa and gives her figure the old predatory look. Time is passing. He'd better make a pass. He really ought to. He stiffens his jaw, reaches his hand out, and puts it over hers in a sudden vise-like clamp. She looks up at him and smiles.*)

ENID. Hello, there.

WORMY. Hi! (*She has not pulled her hand away. This throws him off balance. She is sitting there so quietly. He decides to go a step further. He runs his hand up and down her arm in a quick massaging movement. Again she looks at him and smiles. He is amazed.*) Gosh—you mean you're not going to slug me?

ENID. No.

WORMY. (*Gratefully, joyously, he raises her hand to his lips.*) Bernardine!

ENID. (*She reaches over and caresses his cheek.*) Enid, Ralph!

WORMY. (*This is like a warm, spring rain on the parched ground of his male ego. He feels within himself a sudden peace, a sense of well-being that takes him back to his childhood. He drops her hand.*) Oh, my gosh!

ENID. What's the matter?

WORMY. Look, you're so darned nice, nobody was ever so nice. So I've got to be on the level with you. I'm not what you think I am. I've just got to tell you that.

ENID. (*Pretends amazement.*) Oh!

WORMY. And you—maybe I've been a heel with you, but you're pretty gullible, sugar. You better get smart. Don't you know any better than to believe what any fellow comes up on the street and tells you? You shouldn't bring just any guy up here to your place. Don't you know guys? Well I do and I know how they talk. You better hang around the back room of the

Shamrock if you want to learn about men. Because they're wolves, most guys, and—what am I talking about—I'm just the same as the rest of them.

ENID. I don't think so, Ralph.

WORMY. Oh, you bet your life I am. So you better remember that from now on and be careful. Enid, that was a line I gave you to bring me up here. I'm not from Idaho and I'm not an orphan. I've never been in an orphanage, even on visiting days.

ENID. (*Laughing.*) Now don't be upset. (*She caresses his cheek and smooths his hair with the palm of her hand.*) You're not the first—er—man who has invented a story to tell a woman.

WORMY. And furthermore I'm not leaving for San Francisco tonight to board a destroyer and be gone seven years.

ENID. I'm so glad you're not. (*She continues the caress.*)

WORMY. I've never been to Idaho. I was raised right out here on Benson Parkway.

ENID. (*Laughs softly.*) That doesn't make you a criminal. I know some very nice people who live out on Benson Parkway. (*She takes his chin in her hand.*) Stop being so disturbed. You're young and you are lonely and confused. That part of it is still true. I tell you I understand it all.

WORMY. (*Raising her hand reverently to his lips.*) You're wonderful. Everything wonderful and beautiful, that's you.

ENID. Thank you and you are very, very attractive, Ralph.

WORMY. You can call me my right name from now on too. My name isn't Ralph. You can call me Wormy.

ENID. Wormy! Wormy! How odd!

WORMY. It's a nickname my best friends call me. I hate my own name. It's Buford. Buford Weldy. I was named that on account of my grandfather. He was a Judge around here. Judge Buford. (ENID *sits bolt upright, stunned.* WORMY *does not notice this change.*) He was dead before I was born, but they named me for him anyway. (ENID *rises slowly from the sofa, hand to throat, and walks to the side of the room by the window.*) I've always hated that name, ever since I can remember. But Enid—(*He gets up and goes to her, stands behind her*) that's beautiful.

ENID. (*Walking quickly away.*) Buford—just a minute—

WORMY. Yes.

ENID. I must tell you something too.

WORMY. (*He follows her.*) I've only known you a few minutes and yet everything you say certainly interests me.

ENID. There was something I didn't tell you.

WORMY. What? Are you married?

ENID. Not any more.

WORMY. So your name isn't Enid. I don't mind.

ENID. (*Her back to him.*) When you told me I shouldn't believe the stories men told me who approached me on the street—you were right. And you, Buford, you must not approach older women either—not ever.

WORMY. Listen, sugar, it's different with a fellow—entirely different. What could happen to me?

ENID. (*She faces him. She speaks with tenderness.*) An older woman? She could learn—to adore you—no matter what your name might be.

WORMY. And what's wrong with that—that's perfect.

ENID. (*Shaking her head.*) And she could steal away your youth—make it pass like a dream.

WORMY. But that's what I want! What all the guys want. That is——Bernardine!

ENID. (*With a sudden movement.*) You've got to go—now.

WORMY. (*Shocked.*) Go? But why? You said you didn't mind my handing you that line.

ENID. Buford, you've got to go because—because—promise me something.

WORMY. Sure—what?

ENID. Promise me you'll never mention to your mother you've been up here.

WORMY. My mother! But that's the way I planned it—never to mention it.

ENID. (*Slowly.*) Your mother and I. We've been friends—for years.

WORMY. You—and—Jeepers! (*He sits down—shakes his head.*) Just my luck!

ENID. Oh, perhaps it's just as well for you it was me and not some strange older woman.

WORMY. Listen, sugar, it was just as well for you it was me and not one of MY friends. They're real wolves, those guys!

ENID. And now you see why you must go—right away.

WORMY. (*He rises and goes to her, standing behind her.*) Look, Enid, I don't know much. Maybe I don't know anything, but I do know I've never felt so comfortable with any woman in all my life. I've never been able to talk to a woman before. I've never been so—so happy. It's got nothing to do with HER. Don't kick me out. Don't do that now.

ENID. I must, dear, I must.

WORMY. Let me stay just a little while longer. Let me spend the evening with you. I won't do a thing you don't want me to do, I promise.

ENID. No. I've made it as easy for you as I could. And I have an appointment. Good-by. (*He says nothing but his shoulders sag. He turns and walks slowly to the door.*) Buford! (*He turns.*) Where are you going? (*He shrugs.*) Go find that girl. And if you can't find her, start looking for another one.

WORMY. (*His voice is low. His eyes rest on her face so reproachfully.*) Is there—anyone else like you—anywhere?

ENID. Forget me, Buford, but believe me. Someday you'll find someone—a girl your age—who won't push you away!

WORMY. (*He gives a short, dry, bitter little laugh. And just before he pushes the door open with a savage jab he says—*) Gee—thanks—Mom! (*He is gone.*)

BLACKOUT

ACT TWO

SCENE 2

TIME: *Several hours later, a little after midnight.*

SCENE: *The street.*

The street is empty. The stars above the towers of the high school in the background sparkle in the night. In the distance we hear the sound of boys' voices singing.

On stage in a group, walk the boys, except WORMY *and* OLSON. BEAUMONT, GRINER, *and* CARNEY *wear slacks, sports jackets, and neckties. Since it is Saturday night they have put on their "date" clothes.* FUDGE *is still in the suede jacket.*

They are singing a song of BEAUMONT'S *improvising. It goes something like this:*

"Oh Bernardine, my Bernardine, the Cruds may come, the Cruds may go. But still the Cruddish moonlight beams on those dear Cruds of long ago! Aaaaaa men!"

It is a dreadful song and in a doubtful melody reminiscent of "Genevieve" and yet not that either, a combination of several barbershop chords. But as they come down the street singing, their arms thrown over each other's shoulders—it sounds charming.

A man in a dark hat and coat is walking from the opposite direction. TUB *steps away from the group. The song stops.*

[93]

TUB. (*To man.*) Do you happen to know the way to the Granada Fish Market?

MAN. No I don't. Sorry. (*He tries to go on.*)

TUB. (*Holding him—turns him around in the direction from whence he came.*) Tell you what you do. Go four blocks that way and turn to the left, three blocks right, and you can't miss it. (*As the man resists he gives him a shove and sends him off. The boys all laugh.*)

BEAUMONT. (*Stepping out from the group and addressing them.*) Men it's Saturday night! In the kitchen of the Palms Restaurant there is upon the wall to the left of the door—a cold air blower! Now!

BOYS. Yeah! Yeah!

CARNEY. The chef is always in that kitchen. He stands there right under that blower.

BEAUMONT. The poor fellow! Oh well, has he always played the game fair?

BOYS. NEVAH! (*Linking arms again and singing "Oh Bernardine, my Bernardine" they go down the street and off the stage.*) (*Following them but cautiously keeping at a distance, come* GIBBS, *pushing his bicycle, and* MC ELROY. *They cross slowly, doggedly, humming the same strange tune in a low note. They are gone and the stage darkens.*)

ACT TWO

SCENE 3

TIME: *A few minutes later.*

SCENE: *The Weldy living room again.*

We see KINSWOOD *sitting by a table, his school books spread out before him. Through a straw he is pulling on a root-beer float. There are two empty glasses with broken straws on the table also. The dog lies on the floor.*

RUTH WELDY *enters in great excitement. She is wearing a dinner dress of brown satin, carrying an evening bag and her fox fur over her arm.*

RUTH. Vernon, have you heard anything?

KINSWOOD. No, Mrs. Weldy. Didn't you find him in Arthur Beaumont's basement?

RUTH. The house was dark. There's nobody home at the Griners' either. (*She goes over and picks up the telephone book.*) Where does that Friedelhauser boy live. What's his father's name?

KINSWOOD. I don't know, Mrs. Weldy. Mother was asking me that the other day.

RUTH. I'm terribly worried, Vernon. He didn't call or anything?

KINSWOOD. Nobody called but the Climax Laundry wanting to know if they could send a couple of men out to pick up the sheets.

RUTH. Pick up the sheets at this time of night! The Climax people know better than that.

KINSWOOD. I thought it was rather strange. He asked for you, but before that he asked for Wormy.

RUTH. Oh—that was that Carney boy. He's always acting smart like that on the telephone. Vernon! If they've been calling here for him then he isn't with them. Where can he be? Vernon! (*She walks over to him.*) Is there anything about Buford I don't know?

KINSWOOD. Why, no, Mrs. Weldy, I don't think so. Except of course you know he is girl crazy.

RUTH. Vernon Kinswood, are you telling me Buford Weldy is girl crazy? Oh no.

KINSWOOD. Well, he has that reputation. I thought you knew that.

RUTH. I didn't dream. Vernon, that only proves what I've always said. You get the reputation of the people you go around with. No matter what Carney said about the laundry I'm going out to the Rancho and look for them. You stay here. Mavis Griner and Dorothy Beaumont promised to call here if they heard where he was. I'll be back when I've found him—and not until then—(*She goes out quickly.*)

KINSWOOD. (*He shrugs and returns to his books and his root-beer float. The telephone rings.*) Hello. No, Buford isn't here. His mother has just gone out to look for him. Is this Mrs. Beaumont? Mrs. Griner? Would you care to leave a message? No? Well, listen! If this should turn out to be Len Carney, you haven't fooled me one bit. (*Slams up receiver angrily.* WORMY *enters the room. His head is lowered, his hands are in his*

[96]

pockets. He is walking slowly, thoughtfully. He nods to VERNON, *goes over and stands by the window.*)

KINSWOOD. About time you showed up. Your mother is crazy. Where have you been?

WORMY. Oh—just around, walkin' around.

KINSWOOD. Weldy, it's time you saw the light.

WORMY. (*With a sigh.*) I think I have. (*He sits down, leans over and picks up the dog, holding him in his arms and petting him.*)

KINSWOOD. Carney just called you. (*This doesn't seem to interest* WORMY *much. Nothing seems to interest him at all.*)

WORMY. Carney, eh? Oh yes, I was supposed to file a report with them on a deal I was working on but I'm filing no report. I don't even know where they are.

KINSWOOD. They're not in Beaumont's basement. Your mother looked. Say, I hear they pull some pretty raw stuff over there. I hear Beaumont sneaks liquor from his old man's cellar. You'd think he'd have a little more feeling for his old man.

WORMY. (*Wearily.*) Listen, Kinswood, I know Beaumont better than you do. The one person in the world he's got plenty of feeling for is his old man. It's the only thing he never cracks wise about, never even talks about. All the guys know that about Beaumont.

KINSWOOD. He has some fine way of showing it.

WORMY. (*A half wistful sad smile plays over his face. His tone is reminiscent and nostalgic as though he were talking about a world now lost to him.*) Beau's got a record collection—what a collection, sweet and hot, bebop and long hair. I never knew a guy so crazy about music.

KINSWOOD. That Griner is a crude specimen. Thinks he's a wolf, but he's a lazy bum.

WORMY. (*Patiently.*) Listen, Kinswood, Griner is a wolf and he's not a lazy bum. He worked nights all last year in a garage to buy his clothes. His old man had to give up his law practice on account of a brain operation.

KINSWOOD. Well, I didn't know that about Griner. I sympathize with anybody's got illness in the family.

WORMY. (*Wistful again.*) Those bull sessions in Beau's basement and the Shamrock. There isn't anything they don't talk about; politics, jet planes, dames, and God.

KINSWOOD. God! Those guys talk about God—they've got a nerve.

WORMY. (*With great feeling.*) Gee, I've had a lot of fun with those guys. I've had more fun with those guys than I ever had in my life.

KINSWOOD. But where will they end? There isn't one of them will ever amount to a damn.

WORMY. I don't think they even plan on it.

KINSWOOD. You've got to keep on the beam in this world.

WORMY. (*He sighs.*) You're right, Vern. You've got the right idea. You stay on the beam, you get along with your folks. You never give a thought to dames. That's the way to be all right. (WORMY *again pets the dog. He has made his deal with himself. Homework, the dog, and* KINSWOOD.)

KINSWOOD. (*He has turned around slowly in his chair and is gaping at* WORMY *in amazement.*) Me—never give a thought to dames? You crazy? I give 'em plenty of thought. (WORMY's *mouth drops open.* KINSWOOD *gets up and walks to him.*) I've given it plenty of thought and I got it all figured out. Do you know a fellow in town named R. L. Pomfrey?

WORMY. (*Nods.*) An old guy?

KINSWOOD. (*He nods.*) About thirty-five. He drives a yellow Jaguar. And those girls that ride with him—are they dreams—are they gorgeous! He's got the prettiest girls in town. When he walks in a restaurant with 'em everybody turns around to stare. Sometimes he has two or three—

WORMY. Yeah? No kiddin!

KINSWOOD. When Pomfrey was in school I hear he didn't date at all. He didn't have a car, didn't have any dough. But he kept sluggin' 'til he got out of school and got established in his profession. Then he got this Jaguar. He's got a place in the mountains for week ends and an apartment in town. He can have anybody he wants—now. (KINSWOOD *leans back against the sofa, his legs sprawled.*) I'll paint my Jaguar maroon color. These snoot-faced girls like Hobbs and Johnson and Cantrick who wouldn't look at me now—they'll be glad to look at me then. But I won't look at them. Because by that time they'll be old and washed up and I'll drive by with a car load of beauties. (*There is a vindictive smile on his face and his eyes glow.*)

WORMY. (*His tone is full of astonishment.*) Cantrick old! I can't imagine Cantrick—ever growing old! (*He looks at* KINSWOOD *with a sudden wave of revulsion.*) Kinswood—you slob! (*He jumps to his feet, runs swiftly to the door, and is gone before* KINSWOOD *can open his mouth.*)

BLACKOUT

ACT TWO

SCENE 4

TIME: *Immediately following.*

SCENE: *The Shamrock.*

As the lights come up we hear the sound of symphonic music. BEAUMONT *sits at the table, his long legs sprawled in front of him, his neck resting on the back of the chair.* FUDGE *is perched on the top of the booth.* CARNEY *stands, one foot on a chair, a beer glass in his hand.* TUB *is leaning against the wall.*

TUB. Tchaikovsky! Wow! He does it to me.

CARNEY. (*He shakes his head.*) He doesn't do it to me.

TUB. You're crazy! Maybe you haven't got anything for him to do it *to!*

CARNEY. (*Frowning.*) Watch it, Griner!

TUB. Okay! Ask Beau.

BEAUMONT. (*He rises and walks back and forth thoughtfully. As always when* BEAUMONT *discusses music he is very serious.*) This guy! (*He indicates the jukebox with a jerk of his thumb.*) He gets down, way, way down—in the muck. Chopin is my boy. He keeps it up there, light and floating—on the top—of the water.

[101]

CARNEY. Don't let this get around but my old man likes Victor Herbert. (*Enter* WORMY. *He looks uneasy, nervy, strained. This is his last visit to the Shamrock but he will say no direct farewell. He has been saying farewell to the boys all evening as he walked around town by himself. But his actual leave-taking must be masked and casual, according to the rules.* CARNEY *sees him first.*) Hey, Weldy, you should have been with us. We went by the Palms Restaurant. Beau kept the chef talking and we reversed the exhaust fan—a forty mile gale blew through that dining room—blew hats, napkins, butter, soup, spaghetti—

WORMY. Kid stuff! (*He faces them.*) Why don't you guys grow up? (*This is a thunderbolt!*)

TUB. (*After a moment of dreadful silence.*) Big crowd at the Rancho tonight, Beaumont?

BEAUMONT. What? Oh yes, pretty good crowd, college crowd.

CARNEY. You have a date with Johnson, Beau?

BEAUMONT. Oh, I was going out there anyway and she wanted to come—so—we worked it out.

CARNEY. We went to the Bee-hive. Weenie Wilson was there with a sharp lookin' babe.

BEAUMONT. I've seen her. She is a lovely creature—long black hair—falling from the nostrils.

WORMY. (*He is standing apart from the gang. Now he clears his throat and tries to make his voice sound very casual.*) I—we— I mentioned the Rancho to my date but she said—"Oh—let's not—too crowded." (*The boys register but act as though they have not heard the interruption.*)

TUB. Afterward we went to that spaghetti place on Alvarado. Ever go there, Beau?

BEAUMONT. Used to—not lately.

[102]

WORMY. We—ah—finally ended up at her place.

FUDGE. (*And how they glare at him.*) You have a date tonight, Wormy?

BEAUMONT. (*At* FUDGE.) Shh——!

CARNEY. I don't see how Weenie rates a date like that.

WORMY. Gosh, but this apartment of hers was swanky, carpets that thick and what do you call those things that hang from the ceiling?

BEAUMONT. (*Drily.*) Meat hooks?

WORMY. Crystal things. This was a gorgeous place, gorgeous.

BEAUMONT. (*With sudden fierce movement. The chair he has had tipped back on two legs now hits the floor with a clack.*) So, you had a big evening, Weldy? Okay, take the platform. Was it tender? Was it real?

WORMY. (*He flicks the ash of his cigarette and pretends an ease he does not feel.*) Oh well, you guys all know how those things are. You've all been around plenty—you claim. (*The boys look at him. It was hard to take anyway, seeing* WELDY *walk off with that beautiful woman, but for him—*WELDY—*of all people to return and strut like this! Doesn't he remember who they are? They're the guys who knock themselves out trying to get dates for him. All eyes, even* BEAUMONT'S, *grow cold.*)

TUB. Us? Oh no, Weldy. You've got us wrong. You're the big wheel!

WORMY. (*Oblivious of the reaction.*) Say, tell me something. Why do they always want to start planning the future? When do I see you again—Monday, Wednesday, Friday? Why won't they let an evening be an evening? (BEAUMONT *is studying him curiously even though coldly, but* TUB *walks over to him with mock solemnity, lays a hand on his arm in fatherly fashion.*)

[103]

TUB. Weldy, you'll just have to start carrying a wet towel—smack them in the face with it—it stings.

CARNEY. Or else rocks. I used to carry big heavy rocks myself but I got so I was all bent over.

BEAUMONT. The boy's got a tough problem. He needs help. Personally, my heart is breaking for him.

WORMY. Aw, cut it. Can't take it, huh? Well, okay—I'll be shovin'—(*But before he can move* OLSON *enters wearing a dinner jacket. He looks pained and shamed, a foolish grin on his face. The boys all laugh, glad of this note of relief.*)

BEAUMONT. Waiter—there you are—right here, waiter—menu please!

OLSON. (*He grins good-naturedly.*) I was dragged. I was framed.

BEAUMONT. You make a mighty pretty picture, Fofo—

OLSON. You don't know the worst. My old man not only made me go out there to the country club tonight with him and my old lady—but they made me take a date—a drip—my sister! (*All the boys laugh loudly—even* WORMY. OLSON *turns to him.*) And Wormy. Your friend was out there too. She was with some old pot!

WORMY. That so? Well—it's late—I'll be shovin'— (*Starts out.*)

CARNEY. (*He jumps up.*) Wait a minute, Weldy! Who did you say was out there, Dink?

OLSON. The blonde he picked up in the hotel. And this old guy with her was even tryin' to dance. He was counting, I swear it—one, two, three—turn—(*The boys have stopped listening to* OLSON. *Every eye is on* WORMY.)

TUB. (*To* CARNEY.) Why do they always want to plan the future? When will I see you again? Sunday, Monday, or never?

CARNEY. But this place of hers—it was so gorgeous!

[104]

BEAUMONT. All those crystal meat hooks!

TUB. And how I had to battle—to get away—

WORMY. (*His face flushes with shame and anger. He clenches his fists.*) Shut up. Cut it—cut it—okay, she took me up there but she threw me out. She turned out to be a friend of my old lady's. So what? Any guy that makes another crack at me— I'll clean him—

TUB. (*Advancing to him, his voice low but dangerous.*) What's that?

BEAUMONT. (*He has been watching* WORMY's *face.*) Tub, shut up!

WORMY. (*Desperately.*) Look, I guess I've got to tell you. My old lady is right about you guys and me. But as usual, she's right for the wrong reasons. I'm just not up to you—that's all. So I'll never be a big wheel or a smooth operator. I'll never make it. I learned that tonight.

BEAUMONT. (*Angry.*) What are you dribbling about? Everybody gets kicked out. Can't you take it? Besides—she was a friend of your old lady's.

CARNEY. That's no reason to go crazy.

WORMY. (*He is running his hands through his hair in agony.*) That's not the point. But I can figure myself—finally. I told her my name. I didn't have to do that but I did it—why? Because I haven't got the wolf teeth—that's why. And if **you** haven't got them you never get them. (*He drops his head. But he says it. Says it out loud, the dreadful admission. It is wrung from him in agony.*) I'm a chicken, that's all. A natural-born chicken. (*Nobody speaks. They are all shocked and shamed by this confession, and no one more than* BEAUMONT. *Because it is like a taunting whisper torn from the depths of his own heart. How many times has he told the same thing to himself—but only to himself. A guy should never say a thing like that out loud.*) (WORMY's *head comes up with a jerk. He glares at them,* *his fists raised.*) If any of you want to do anything about that—come on. I'll slug the first guy tries to tell me I'm not a chicken. (*But nobody speaks or moves—except* WORMY. *He starts for the door, gets there, and turns.*) So long you guys—good luck—and I mean good luck. (*They make no answer. They are all watching him. Suddenly off stage from the doorway at the other side of the room there is heard the sound of a voice calling—*"Buford—Buford." WORMY *stops where he is. Enter* RUTH WELDY, *her head high, her face flushed. Her heels make a sharp clicking sound as she walks to the center of the room. She pulls a paper out of her purse, hands it to* BEAU.)

RUTH. Take a look at that! Show it to Marvin. Show it to Leonard. Pass it around. Thirty-five on his last Math exam and then you wonder why I'm nearly crazy. You've all got some pretty advanced ideas. Oh, I'm not blind, boys, but I can't fight you alone any longer. Arthur, I'm going to your father the first thing in the morning.

WORMY. (*Horrified.*) Oh, Mother—don't!

RUTH. (*Tight-lipped.*) Buford, I heard you tell these boys this morning you had homework over the week end. Then they persisted in dragging you down here this afternoon—and to-night too.

WORMY. Mother—they didn't drag me down here. I came myself.

RUTH. (*Her tone to him is gentler.*) It's nice of you to defend your friends, dear, but I know better. That's why I'm going to Arthur's father.

WORMY. (*In a panic.*) But look, Beau's old man doesn't care a thing about where I go.

RUTH. (*Turning back to* BEAU.) But I do. Arthur, your father is the finest and the kindest man in this town; and one of the wisest. (BEAU's *face has turned white but his head is up, his eyes looking into hers with a cool contempt.* WELDY's *old lady trying to tell him anything about his old man!*) He'll help me. I know he will. It's time he realized a few of the things that are going on. (*She walks toward the door.*) Come on, Buford. I'm parked sideways in that parking lot. You'll have to get me out. (*But* WORMY *has not moved. She gets to the door, then turns and sees him, standing like a rock.*) Buford, are you coming?

WORMY. (*Across the length of the room he faces her. Between them stand the boys, in a group.*) No.

RUTH. Well, when are you coming?

WORMY. Never.

RUTH. Buford, stop this. Let's not have a family scene right here. Come on.

WORMY. No.

RUTH. (*Patiently.*) If you're not coming home with me—where may I ask—are you going?

WORMY. I'm going—to join the navy. (*The stillness in the room seems to deepen as* RUTH *gasps at her son. His jaw is like granite. His eyes are steely. Slowly he takes his draft registration card out of his pocket and hits it against his hand.*) And nobody can stop me! (RUTH *realizes in this moment that this is a young man, not a child any longer, and that what he says is true. She shakes her head woefully—a little cry leaps from her throat.*)

RUTH. Darling! (*She goes to him slowly, places her hand timidly on his shoulder. Her voice is gentle, bewildered.*) Oh darling! (*He stands rigid.*) Darling!

BEAUMONT. (*Clearing his throat.*) Don't blow your top, Weldy!

RUTH. (*She grasps at a straw.*) There—you heard what Arthur said—that's right, Arthur!

TUB. You'll be in the service soon enough, Weldy.

RUTH. (*She is stroking his arm, petting him, soothingly.*) You heard Marvin. Your friends know you have to graduate. You listen to them. Boys, (*She turns to them*) try talking some sense into him. My! I guess we're all a little on edge tonight. You stay right here and visit with your friends. I'll get the car out myself. (*Hurriedly, frightened, hoping she has repaired the damage, she starts to go quickly toward the door—half running.*)

WORMY. (*In a low tone to* BEAU.) I don't think she'll go to your old man now, Beau. (*With a quick movement he goes to the exit at the other side of the room and is gone.*)

CARNEY. Weldy—where you goin'?

RUTH. (*Running back to the boys in panic.*) Boys—Arthur! Don't let him go! Go after him! Talk to him! Please!

BEAUMONT. Leave him alone, Mrs. Weldy.

RUTH. (*She seems to sag.*) I suppose I'll have to. (*Bitterly.*) It's all Jean Cantrick's fault! Buford has always liked her and I'd hoped that deep down she liked him even though she's been dreadful to him lately. I would be perfectly happy if something came of that—perfectly happy. (*She walks to the door and puts her hand on the knob. Then she stops. The boys are watching her. She walks slowly back to them. When she speaks her voice is full of awe.*) Why no I wouldn't! I wouldn't be happy at all. Not at all. (*She looks at them.*) Oh what's the matter with us? Nothing in creation is good enough for you— nothing and no one. We don't want you to live the way we've lived, love the way we've loved, or die the way we'll die. We want the miracle! We want you to walk into the future a brand new way—over a bridge of rainbows! (*The boys are horribly embarrassed over this emotional outburst. Each drops his eyes.*) You didn't know that, did you Arthur? (*She lays a*

hand on his arm.) You, Marvin? (*She looks at* TUB.) **Or you,**
Leonard? (*Now at* CARNEY.) Well, I could never have said that
to Buford either. Good night, boys. (*She walks slowly to the
door.*)

BEAUMONT. (*With difficulty.*) Mrs. Weldy— (*She turns.*)
Couldn't I—get your car out for you?

RUTH. (*Shakes her head sadly.*) You stay here—all of you—as
long as you can. (*She looks wonderingly around the grimy,
dirty old room and then goes out.*) (*They are all silent.*)

OLSON. (*Finally.*) Jeepers! Imagine Weldy, on a bridge of rainbows—chasin' a dame.

FUDGE. (*In a wondering tone.*) Weldy, standin' up to his old lady
like that—I didn't think he'd ever do it.

BEAUMONT. And I never thought I'd ever feel sorry for Mrs.
Weldy.

TUB. The look on her face when he said he was joining the navy.
That was perfect.

BEAUMONT. (*Jumping up. He must put on his comic mask again.
He walks like a professor giving a class lecture.*) Oh, it was
good, but it was not perfect. Now up in Sneaky Falls—it's the
mothers who join the navy and the boys run like crazy mailing
them boxes of raisin cookies. Say—how about a round of beer—
(*Slaps the table.*) Helen—Service—Service—(*They all begin
to stamp their feet yelling—*"Service—Service.")

HELEN. (*She comes in on the run. She wears a coat over her green
uniform, carries her pad and pencil in her hand.*) Don't race
your motor. Cut that out. I just come back on duty. Okay—
(*She counts them—writes it down on the pad.*) Say—which
one of you is Weldy—?

BEAUMONT. None of us. We are all named Bidnut. Weldy's gone—
to the navy. Why do you ask?

HELEN. (*Taking a paper out of her pocket.*) Some dame's been callin' him here—all evening.

TUB. (*To the others.*) His old lady. (*To* HELEN.) She found him.

HELEN. Then he knows about it.

TUB. He knows about it. (HELEN *takes the slip of paper out her pocket, wads it up, and throws it on the floor.*)

HELEN. She called about eight-thirty—at nine, and then just before I went off duty at ten-thirty. She sure seemed anxious. Cantrick —that's a funny name. I had to make her spell it—(*She goes out. They all make one leap for the crumpled paper.* BEAU *gets it.*)

CARNEY. Cantrick calling Weldy—must be a gag!

FUDGE. She never calls anybody. She's too stuck up.

TUB. Cantrick calling Weldy—never.

OLSON. Ernie Cook's kid sister and the Lamson girls, they're always calling up guys and giving phony names. They're about fourteen.

BEAUMONT. (*He has now smoothed out the paper and studies it.*) No—listen. Ask him to call Miss Jean Cantrick—right away. MISS Jean Cantrick—that's Cantrick—(*He jumps to his feet and begins giving orders like an army officer directing a charge.*) Carney—go to the Blue Goose—(CARNEY *runs out quickly.*) Olson, make for the Black Cow. Tub, try the Beehive. Fudge, come with me—we'll go to the Rancho. (*Galvanized into action they are all grabbing for their coats.*)

TUB. He never goes to the Bee-hive. He likes the drive-in on Eighth!

OLSON. The Black Cow closes at eleven.

BEAUMONT (*Racing for his coat.*) Try them—get movin'—stop

stallin'—give it the gun! (*They are heading for the door in a wild rush—when who should enter but* WORMY, *followed by* CARNEY. WORMY *has his necktie off, his hair is rumpled. He carries his coat over his arm. He looks beaten and weary, in contrast to their excitement.*)

CARNEY. He was right outside—sitting on the curbing.

WORMY. (*Suspicious.*) Is this a frame? Is my mother behind this?

BEAUMONT. No. Carney, look up that number.

WORMY. (*Going to the phone.*) I know that number. (*He dials it wearily. He has no hope of anything, not in this world.*) Hello, Jean. This is Buford Weldy. (*He covers the mouthpiece and turns to the boys, who have grouped tightly around the telephone. There is an amazed look on his face.*) Shh—she says she's been calling me all evening. Where have I been?

BEAUMONT. You're sorry you missed her. You've been—around.

WORMY. Sorry I missed you. Oh—around. (*Again to boys.*) She says she went to the dance at the Wilmore Country Club.

BEAUMONT. She wants you to ask her who she went with—humor the babe.

WORMY. (*Still wary.*) Who'd you go with? Some other girl? Oh, you went with Pete Langley—well, that's the same thing.

BEAUMONT. (*With a raised eyebrow at the gang.*) Just listen to us chickens!

WORMY. (*In quick, hushed tone to them.*) She tried to call me from there too. She's been worried about me. (*Into phone.*) You mustn't worry about me—doll. (*To boys.*) She still wants to know what I did this evening. Shall I tell her the truth, Beau?

BEAUMONT. I wouldn't. But that's up to you, Fofo—entirely up to you.

WORMY. (*Listening at phone again.*) Aw, Jean—now, look, Jean
—(*To boys.*) Hey, blow—will you. (*They retreat quickly out
of the door.* WORMY's *voice becomes intimate and tender.*)
Look, Jean, why everybody knows you're the sharpest kid in
town. Why wouldn't Langley act like a stinker? He's just an
old pot. Now, Jean, don't cry. Please, Jean. Everybody gets
a bum break once in a while. That's life, youngster. What?
Maybe I can. I'll try to make it. (*Slowly he hangs up. His face
is dazed still; dazed with an unbelievable happiness. Then he
shouts.*) Fellas—fellas—(*The boys have been waiting outside
the door. They run back in.*) Say-ay—Cantrick is all alone up
there. She feels like a hamburger. Could I borrow your car,
Tub?

TUB. (*Tosses him the keys.*) The wheel—the winnah! (*The boys
rush over, pick him up, raise him high above their shoulders,
while he struggles but grins happily all the while. They carry
him out triumphantly—crying out:* "The wheel—the winnah—
make way for the wheel!")

*   *   *

*After they've gone, we can hear their voices dying away out-
side while the jukebox plays on in the empty, shabby room.
This time it is a piece of rakish bebop. It seems to be calling
them back. They don't come and the curtain slowly falls.*

*But the house lights don't come on. What's the trouble? Isn't
the play over? Again the pin spotlight moves across the velvet
and here is* BEAUMONT *again in his Air Force uniform. Of
course!* BEAU *must always have the last word. He gives that
nonchalant piano-playing wave. He says:*

"So we gave Weldy an escort up there that night, almost a
police escort. We were stopped twice by the cops for sounding
our horns and trying to keep formation.

"He decided on the way up there he wouldn't tell Cantrick anything—except how he felt about her.

"There's a new King at the Shamrock today and maybe even another confused kid like Wormy, trying to be a wheel. I hope he makes it. My old gang has gone. But wherever THEY are or whoever HE is—I'd like to sign this whole thing—Best Regards from Beaumont!"

He steps back behind the curtains and now the play is over!